Through the Church Door

Through the Church Door

HAROLD P. SIMONSON

WIPF & STOCK · Eugene, Oregon

THROUGH THE CHURCH DOOR

Copyright © 2010 Harold P. Simonson. All rights reserved. Except for brief quotations in critical publications or reviews, no part of this book may be reproduced in any manner without prior written permission from the publisher. Write: Permissions, Wipf and Stock Publishers, 199 W. 8th Ave., Suite 3, Eugene, OR 97401.

Wipf & Stock
An Imprint of Wipf and Stock Publishers
199 W. 8th Ave., Suite 3
Eugene, OR 97401
www.wipfandstock.com

ISBN 13: 978-1-1-60899-064-1

Manufactured in the U.S.A.

The Scripture quotations contained herein are from the Revised Standard Version of the Bible, copyright 1952 [2nd edition, 1971] by the Division of Christian Education of the National Council of the Churches of Christ in the United States of America. Used by permission. All rights reserved.

To my loving wife Carolyn, our children, and grandchildren; to my daughter-in-law Erin Simonson for her generous assistance time and again; to Steve Wilson who made the cross in colored glass that hangs at my study window and comes alive with each day's dawn; and to the memory of Bob Albertson, a friend of nearly fifty years, who first invited me to share in Christian ministry.

*And there is a Catskill eagle in some souls that can
alike dive down into the blackest gorges,
and soar out of them again and become invisible
in the sunny spaces.*

Herman Melville, *Moby-Dick*

*Behold, I stand at the door and knock; if any one
hears my voice and opens the door, I will come in
to him and eat with him, and he with me.*

Revelation 3:20

Contents

Preface ix
Opening xi

1 Transitions 1
2 Words 10
3 Home 26
4 Communion 39
5 Tragedy 55
6 Age 77
7 Grace 93

Closing 103

Preface

THE GOVERNING metaphor of this book is the "door" which opens and closes but signifies a deeper level: outside/inside; objective/subjective; secular/sacred. Theology, implicit throughout, reveals a minister's experiences both inside and outside the church. I see his calling as living in both at once, thus the paradox that develops as the chapters unfold.

Paradoxes can be puzzling. Jesus' disciples found them so. It is not easy to hold two opposed ideas in the mind at the same time. In startling analogy Herman Melville marveled at a whale's brain—how it reconciles simultaneously two opposing prospects, one eye on one side and the other in an exactly opposite direction. Such is the novelist's way of illustrating what we experience when, for example, we confront many New Testament paradoxes: tragedy as separation / divine comedy as reconciliation; this world and the next; light and darkness; birth/death/rebirth. Personally, as my own age lengthens I see life itself not in terms of either/or but paradoxically both/and.

In this book I seek to extend the reader's imagination and quicken sensibility beyond the restrictions imposed by scholarly research and citation. I allude to literary writers as well as biblical. References are self-explanatory, thus the absence of footnotes and bibliography. My style is informal, anecdotal, threaded with ruminations pertaining to both sides of the church door. I intend the book for a general audience, not specialized, but intelligent and informed. Personal thoughts and experiences provide the documentation.

Opening

THESE REFLECTIONS owe their origin to two stints I served (a total of twenty-one months) as interim minister at a Congregational Church. The first period answered a friend's invitation to join him as co-minister. He was a retired professor of religion and an ordained Methodist, and I, an emeritus professor of English after a forty-year career. But when, after nine months for family reasons he resigned, I was ordained according to Church polity and assumed the necessary duties during the remaining five months.

The new fulltime minister's tenure lasted a short three years. After his departure I again filled in, this time for the six-month period that frames this book. It was then I recognized a drumbeat sounding a summons different from the one before.

To repeat, this second interim extended from July through winter's darkest days. Besides the weekly sermon, I led a Sunday morning adult study class and a Wednesday noontime prayer and meditation service; officiated at memorial services, weddings, and christenings; served the Communion bread and cup; made home and hospital visits; attended church council and committee meetings; and represented the church at community events. When the next full-time minister arrived, I relinquished my duties and became a Hospice chaplain and later joined Tacoma's Nightwatch ministry serving patrons in downtown taverns.

I was past sixty-five, a time when a person had better get serious about something more than golf. I resolved to make retirement a new beginning, a trajectory upward to counter the one that nature unambiguously curves downward. My first sermon coincided with a Fourth of July Sunday. Summer gave way to autumn and then to bleak midwinter.

Years before, I had attended a New Year's Day vesper service in London's Westminster Abbey. My chair rested on a stone slab sealing the bones of someone whose name and elegiac inscription chiseled into the stone had been worn away. Also gone were the dates of birth and death. The only markings I could make out were "Born" and "Died." On that cold evening the priest's voice reinforced these two universal truths forever conjoined.

We can do nothing about our birth and the factual certainty of death. However, early on I entered what my mother called the "age of accountability." Back then I assumed she meant adulthood, but no, she sternly meant the present and, of course, my awakening adolescence. She insisted on self-appraisal according to norms of duty, effort, and morality. Her quiet ways, indeed her love, added authority to her expectations. Even now I hear her voice compelling me to look inward, and if there is guilt, then pray for forgiveness—if darkness, wait patiently for the light.

What in my youth seemed always changing, always becoming, now reveals a different pattern, not in terms of "ages" (Shakespeare designates seven, starting with the infant's "mewling and puking" and ending with "mere oblivion" of old age: "sans teeth, sans eyes, sans taste, sans everything, *As You Like It*, II, vii 129–166) but now embracing both time and timelessness. This pattern consists of certain markers. When thought turns to meditation, I detect seven hallmarks—chapter titles—identifying who I am and where I find truth to live by: Transitions, Words, Home, Communion, Tragedy, Age, Grace. In some strange way these words bore special gravitas each time I opened or closed the church door: a two-way passage—entrance and exit—inside and outside—sacred and secular.

1

Transitions

Having taught and preached, I'm prepared to contrast the two. For nearly forty years I took my comfortable place in the university classroom, usually positioned behind a lectern but sometimes sidling over to a window or stepping back to scribble on the chalkboard. I enjoyed "drawing" my ideas, making little circles and then connecting them with sturdy lines, adding arrows pointing this way or that and Xs here and there. The lecture finished and the students out the door, I erased the lines and circles so cunningly conceived, a courtesy extended to the next hour's instructor who did the same after his allotted time.

After I re-stuffed my briefcase to leave, a student or two would sometimes stroll alongside me to my office where we'd probe further into the poem, novel, play, or essay. Perhaps the English major asked why Emily Dickinson's opening line seems so benign yet frightening: "Because I could not stop for Death— / He kindly stopped for me"? Or what's the difference between Ahab's madness and Pip's in *Moby-Dick*? Or how Jonathan Edwards reconciled divine wrath and mercy in his New England writings. Long years of classroom teaching, while always challenging, exhausted me. Yet after retirement I still wanted something more.

I need to explain that my university career had allowed me sabbatical leaves during which I chose seminary study at Princeton, Yale, and the University of St. Andrews, Scotland, where in the early 1970s I earned a BPhil in Divinity. My thesis (later published) was on Jonathan Edwards. This degree, plus a previous Northwestern University doctorate in English and specialization in seventeenth- and eighteenth-century American religious thought, supported the church deacons' recommendation that I be ordained. I submitted a required "Spiritual Autobiography" to the regional Vicinage Council, which questioned me on several points before signing approval. I was ordained April 24, 1994, the 106th birthday of my deceased father. "Most unusual," said several Council members noting my white hair.

Most sobering too, as I processed down the center aisle each Sunday morning, the choir robed in royal blue and I in black to take my place in the pulpit and call the people to worship . . . to read the Scripture . . . pray and preach and speak words of benediction, and again to follow the choir up the aisle while the organist pulled out all the stops for the recessional.

This was no lecture hall. The aesthetics were all different: stained glass diffusing sunlight; sloping, converging symmetry of aisles and pews; the open Bible centered on the Communion table and the cross on the wall behind; the music, the silence, the sanctuary. The congregation was different too: not the irrepressible young but the aged and scarred who had journeyed far out and in. Their concerns were not exams and grade-point averages, but healing and its consolations; not visions of money and career, but God's kingdom.

Along with these differences were others: explaining/proclaiming, analyzing a poem / praying for insight to unlock a gospel parable or Pauline paradox. Unlike lecturing, preaching left me more exposed, resembling the difference between entering a library and a hospital, between reading a book and sitting with the sick, injured, and dying.

Teaching had been an exhilarating vocation, the more complex the more challenging. But something else energized preaching, something beyond intellect and more akin to the heart mysteriously touched by the rule of love.

Years before, I had been drawn to the writings of medieval mystics and the ambience of Gothic cathedrals. Even earlier I had spent time trekking from monastery to monastery built a thousand years ago on the Mount Athos peninsula in Greece, and seeking intimations of Eastern Orthodox spirituality. As I neared sixty, I began responding to J. S. Bach, truly awakening one bone-cold January evening in frozen Edinburgh to the spiritual power infusing his Mass in B Minor.

A strange thing happened that confirmed what Julian of Norwich had said in her classic *Revelations of Divine Love*: "So it was [she wrote] that I learned that love was our Lord's meaning. And I saw for certain, both here and elsewhere, that before ever he made us, God loved us; and that his love has never slackened, nor ever shall." When the Bach performance ended, I tightened my scarf and hurried home along Princes Street, striking my heels in ringing cadence to the words, "In God's love we have our beginning."

Teaching abjures subjective experience smacking of religion, but in my later classroom years I came close to interjecting religion when trying to pry undergraduates open to these matters of importance, matters that all great literature addresses. I expected students to have had some relevant nascent experiences if only to ask an occasional question. In the assumption I forgot my forty-year advantage. Nevertheless, I grew impatient with the glibness and easy generalizations that layered their papers. I wanted gritty ideas that attacked home-grown assumptions. The gap between lectern and the front row grew too broad for leaping, another way of saying that as I was aging they remained forever young, each year's new class the same.

Unlike teaching, preaching is proclamation. Its content is the kerygma (*keryssein*: proclaim), the gospel's Good News. If preaching is only social and political admonishment; only trendy psychology; only archaeology, anthropology, historical research, instruction in ethics; only rhetorical art, it fails its purpose. Preaching involves the human heart responding to one's own will and to God's.

The pulpit is a special place. In *Moby-Dick* (ch.8) Melville describes the New Bedford chapel with its lofty pulpit shaped like a ship's prow. In this heightened place Father Mapple preaches God's word, "this sure Keel of the Ages." His sermon finished, he remains in the prow to pray from regions of the soul deeper than the ocean itself. The departing parishioners silently pass marble tablets bordered in black and mortared into the chapel walls. That Father Mapple preached as if separate and alone discounts the fact that his eloquence derived from shared experience. He united pulpit and pew in common humanity.

No commemorative tablets remembering whalemen lost at sea weigh upon the walls of this venerable church. However, my pulpit-words carried the same implicit text, *memento mori*. They had nothing to do with academic pedigree, but everything pertaining to the scars common to everyone.

Not for a moment do I denigrate teaching. I labored too long and too happily to do that. From the lectern I introduced students to great literature and drew interpretive patterns helping them in ways they needed. Unfortunately, the allotted time was too brief, only a ten-week term in classes too large for dialogue or, at best, longer periods with graduate students engaged in doctoral research.

My church congregation gave no thought to "higher education." No SAT scores were required to attend and no grade-point average to stay. The people came to pray for grace, not grades, and graduation consisted in knowing God's abiding love. They were shown intersecting lines, one horizontal and one vertical, which no professor's chalkboard explained. The listeners made the difference—the gap between the students beginning their journey and adults nearing the end. Could the church be a "school" for these older sojourners?

In analyzing the relationship between psychology and religion the renowned psychoanalyst Carl Jung observed in *Modern Man in Search of a Soul* that among the aging patients whom he treated the central problem was the absence of a "religious outlook" on life. He puzzled that religion no longer offers schools that prepare the middle-aged "for the second half of life, for old age, death and eternity." The lesson he would have his patients learn is that they cannot live the afternoon of life according to the program of life's morning—"for what was great in the morning will be little at evening, and what in the morning was true will at evening have become a lie."

Metaphorically depicting this contrast is a Japanese garden, its arched bridge spanning a pool of rounded stones. The beginning traveler sees only the apex and the limitless sky beyond. But when arriving at the mid-point and casting his eye ahead and unnecessarily downward, he sees for the first time the end. The world looks different, more restricted. The mind becomes more introspective. Life's pattern takes shape, the beginning trajectory destined for its terminus. A so-called mid-life crisis forces the traveler to assess where he's been and where he's going. In another image, Robert Frost's sky-high birch tree inexorably bends its climber back to the old earth, lacerating him on the way down.

My six-month second interim started with the church doorbell. Standing there that summer morning was Megan, in her early twenties, her cheek bruised below the eye and her forehead scratched and scabby. She needed help fast, some food, and a safe place to stay the night. The court-imposed restraining order had not stopped her "boyfriend" from beating her, and she knew he still lurked close by. I phoned the Social Services director at the Salvation Army who instructed me to bring Megan in. The three of us sat together in her office. Her first words reassured

Megan that she was a person of importance whom God loved. As I reached to hold her hand, she whispered to me, "Do I really have potential? Does God really love me?"—tender questions from one who felt so worthless. Her words resonated as if from the Psalms. The counselor arranged her night's stay in an unnamed shelter known only to the Salvation Army staff. She would be safe there. Down the hallway I heard preparations for lunch. I thanked the social worker for her kindness. I gave Megan a hug and returned through the church door to prepare for an afternoon pre-marriage counseling appointment, plan the upcoming Wednesday noontime prayer and meditation service, and compose Friday's memorial service for a friend.

While reviewing the marriage vows with the young couple, I asked them to repeat their respective parts. Before the session ended I offered two pieces of advice: *first*, when—not if, but when—the marriage hits stormy seas, work it out, tough it out, talk it out, pray it out, love it out, go to a third party for counseling, but never to Mommy and Daddy; *second*, a full life includes something more than married love. Without spiritual luminescence even family love, however successful, is not enough. Life's fullness requires a sense of the holy. In saying this I knew that unless anchored in experience such words quickly float away. I doubted their anchorage but prayed for it nonetheless.

For the Friday memorial service I prepared my words carefully. I recalled what my friend had wanted "when the time came." He said he didn't fear death as much as the embarrassment a paltry attendance at his service would bring to his two sons. He had wanted swing tunes of the 1940s. His family chose Bach Preludes. I spoke about the mystery and wonder of life, of death. Friends and colleagues filled the sanctuary.

Long years before, he and I had hiked countless trails in the Washington Cascade mountains, once standing together atop Mount St. Helens' jagged crater rim. Now he was gone, killed when his red Cherokee spun off a nighttime Idaho freeway. State troopers surmised he had dozed at the wheel. He had been driving home from Utah where he had joined Moab jeepsters in their clubby, motorized quest for desert solitaire. A neurologist, he had purchased personalized license plates sporting the word BRAIN. The accident had crushed his skull. On our last hike he had insisted that neurological synapses explain life. I had said No, that life includes dimensions beyond that. Then death struck.

As for the church neighborhood, the city planners call it "lower middle class," a racial and ethnic mixture blotched by poverty. Across the street from the church the city's hospital occupies an entire triple block. Sirens scream whatever the hour. Across the back alley stands the Christian Science center; its white walls and fluted columns resembling a Greek temple. Chiseled into its cornerstone is LOVE. Its parking lot abuts another belonging to the County Blood Bank, and farther along is a Lutheran church, a food distribution and meal center for the homeless, a five-story brick apartment building, and several rundown houses squeezed side by side dating back to the Depression or earlier. Children's battered tricycles, scooters, and K-Mart plastic toys litter the porches.

Central to the neighborhood is Wright Park. On many July and August days I ate my sack lunch beneath the giant oak where I played as a child. Near several chestnut trees are the same horseshoe pits where my father competed for the city championship. My grandchildren Maria and John fed the ducks and frolicked on the swings and monkey bars. I tried to instruct them about trees: the cypress and hemlock, the sugar and big leaf maples, the scotch elms, the cedars, black locust, birch, and redwoods.

Wedged across the Park was a small Puerto Rican restaurant where I often ordered a veggie sandwich and a cup of peppery soup. One afternoon I lingered longer than usual. The last customer to leave, I asked the owner/waitress about the framed aerial photograph of Chicago. She and her husband, both Puerto Ricans, had lived in Chicago thirty years and reared three sons and two daughters. She proudly showed me snapshots. Her husband had owned a neighborhood grocery store and she a beauty parlor. But at the urging of their eldest son, they'd joined him in Tacoma. Their modest restaurant served Puerto Rican dishes and Chicago-style pizza.

She described her church south of town. Then for unannounced reasons she began deeper talk.

Back in Chicago her marriage had been breaking apart. Both she and her husband had started drinking heavily. Alone one Saturday night while watching TV and holding a third martini, she wondered if her husband would return. He had been gone three days and she didn't know where. She was ready to call it quits, call everything quits: the marriage, the day, the night, everything. The night wore on, her eyes too glazed to follow the cop show and she too tired, too weighted down to click it off. A TV evangelist came on next, speaking words that seemed mere noise. She let him rave.

Suddenly there in the darkness, just the two of them, he looked straight at her and said, "You, you there sitting alone tonight in Chicago and holding a martini in your hand, listen to me." Her dim eyes opened. The voice continued, "God forgives us our sins. God heals. God's spirit can enter empty lives." She slipped to her knees in front of the TV and wept for what seemed a lifetime. That was all she remembered, sprawled on the floor, her face and arms wet with tears.

She said the morning light was like nothing she had ever seen. It filled everything in a new way, not only their bedroom where her husband lay asleep but her whole "insides."

I eyed a New Testament lying next to the spindled receipts. I asked if she had one in English. I shared a passage, the one Paul wrote to the Romans (8:31) about nothing ever separating us from the love of God. Her face glowed and I felt strangely warm too.

That evening I told the story to a friend who teaches philosophy. Analyzing her experience, he rambled something about the "cognitive component of epistemology." "But Jim," I said, "the revelation was mine too. Her light filled me. Isn't that enough? Do we need to know more?" "Yes," he answered, gripping my arm, "it's enough."

Transitions retain their beginnings and endings. Life's waxing and waning make a single curve, the bridge a single span, a paradox. Youthful idealism becomes mature realism including darkness and mystery we dare not scorn or deny. What follows death is not for us to know unless through imagination or intuition we have "a sense sublime / of something far more deeply interfused" (Wordsworth)—or through Christian faith, "a house of many rooms" provided by God who loves us (the gospeler John).

2

Words

SUNDAY SERMONS test honesty. Soon into the second six-month interim I realized again how quickly Sundays come around. For my sermon topics I considered using the published lectionary to simplify selecting a biblical text. With so much else expected during the week, sermons would be easier this way: take the designated lesson; explicate it; avoid big theological words; touch (briefly) upon doctrine; add a homey illustration or two (humor helps); and make closing remarks trenchant. *Voilá*, finished.

But the task didn't work this way. It was good that I remembered the Cathedral of St. Giles in Edinburgh where I worshiped in the mid-1980s. To mount its pulpit the minister climbed semi-circular steps and entered through a low-slung gate. Elevation signified important business in this time-worn bastion of Scottish Calvinism. Before preaching the minister swept his eyes over the congregation. On most Sundays it numbered little more than two hundred, sparse in such a vast and venerable place. Harsh winter mornings brought only a straggling few with rows and rows of interlocking chairs left empty. Would this small number throttle his spirit today?

I wondered what he thought when viewing the motley gathering: how each worshiper had come bearing private hurts and expectations as in a doctor's office, each person sitting alone, waiting. I sensed that this good Scottish minister, who grew up on a wind-lashed island of the Outer Hebrides, would preach from his heart and with no less urgency if only one worshiper had come that day. I trusted his honesty, his diagnosis of the human condition, and the remedy.

In the century-old Tacoma church four carpeted steps approach the chancel and one additional step the pulpit. Of the many times I stood in this place, whatever the attendance, I judged my sermon important and prayers urgent. Empty pews in front and along the side challenged me all the more to reach the people who had come. A lapel microphone supplied the decibels, but for the words themselves I needed power from another source.

My first sermons highlighted Biblical voices heard from the past. Whether or not God had "inspired" them was an issue I left for a different venue. I insisted they were human voices rising from fear, hate, desolation—also from hope, joy, and adoration. Some voices lamented separation from God. Others quaked in confession or burst in rhapsodic praise. Throughout, the biblical words belonged to our brothers and sisters no matter the centuries separating us.

I chose Moses, the Psalmist, Jeremiah, Job, and Paul. Whereas Bible thumpers stress Scripture's inerrant words ("the Bible says")—as if Jeremiah's words no longer belonged to him but to an iconographic object called The Bible—I wanted *his* cries, blasphemies, prayers, and prophecies. I put aside the scholars' quest for historical sources and context. I claimed the right to listen to real voices and tally them with my own. That's the rub that honesty demands.

Trouble comes when we treat the Bible as a literal book, so inviolable that we dare not touch it with soiled hands or scribble along its margins. So awesome is its gravitas, so special its gilt-edged pages, so divine its power that to add a jot or tittle jeopardizes our salvation. I reminded myself that Christianity is a religion not of the book but the *event* informed by the transforming Word best heard in one's deep center.

My mainstay Bible, the Revised Standard Version, is the one I used when teaching my Bible as Literature class at the University of Washington. I make no apologies for the scrawls and scratchings crowding the margins and the heavy underlining in John's gospel and Paul's letter to the Romans. I'm counting on the scotch tape reinforcing its spine and frayed boards to last my remaining years.

In her *Collected Papers*, the English scholar Evelyn Underhill probed what she called "the inside of life." To begin, she tells a story about an American student who had come to England to study his "foreign" inner world. The prescription given him by a London divine was to spend a year, the first half among peasants—"simple, slow-minded, narrow, even superstitious"— practicing their rigid traditional faith; then six months among "alert, cultured, modern intellectuals," cynical about religion and even despising it. Afterward the student must ask himself which of these two groups, if either, had found the secret of how best to meet the crucial realities of life: suffering, joy, passion, love, sin, failure, loneliness, death.

The American spent six months with a German peasant family: devout, narrow, slow-witted, superstitious, always offending his taste. The second half-year he lived among students in Berlin: delightful, intelligent, keen-witted, emancipated from religious prejudices. After returning to England he was asked by his mentor what the peasants know about meeting life's deepest experiences. The American answered, "Everything." And the Berlin students? "They were helpless"—no clue, no inwardness.

For Underhill, the story contrasted the "sharply focused scientific truth," which quickened the university students' minds, and the "dim, deep spiritual truth," which nourished the peasants' souls. The Berliners had no aim or significance beyond themselves and their achievements. By contrast the peasants (uncultured, rough-hewn) harbored an invisible aim ennobling their lives; God and the soul mattered more than anything else. Theirs was profound reverence toward fundamental mysteries of human existence.

Being "twofold" creatures, we live outside and inside. What turns the balance askew? The easy answer is our preoccupation with the outer world of information, current affairs, physical wellbeing, common sense. We hesitate to go within where mysteries swirl like leaves in viewless winds. Yet from these depths (*de profundis*) reverence is born.

Like Underhill, Melville knew the summons: "Hark ye yet again,—the little lower level." He admired persons who "dive deeply"—down into what Augustine in *Confessions* called "a great deep. . . . I dive down deep as I can and I can find no end."

In retirement I have been culling my personal library. A downtown bookstore makes fair deals and what it doesn't want the local Goodwill accepts sans inspection. I also find myself more generous in giving books to friends who show the slightest interest. However, disposing of books that once helped shape my life is a wrenching decision. Saying this, I'm resolved not to clear out everything. Some books continue to have at me. I re-read Melville, Henry James, Emily Dickinson, Faulkner, Eliot—and Jonathan Edwards, who knew *their* inner worlds and helped me know *mine*.

And more: Augustine, Kierkegaard, Dostoevsky, Chekhov, Mann, Camus, Beckett, Hemingway, and certain theologians whom I call the three Bs (Barth, Bultmann, Bonhoeffer) plus Tillich, R. Niebuhr, Thomas Merton, and medieval mystics. Two books I treasure with special affection: first, the *Merriam-Webster New Collegiate Dictionary* (second edition) with my name embossed and still visible on the cover. As a fledgling teaching assistant at Northwestern University fifty years ago, I received a complimentary copy from the M-W company. The other book is my Bible, now over thirty years old.

I've often imagined an evening spent with the biblical John and Paul, gathered, say, with Melville or Camus around the walnut dining table my father made. For its table cloth I'd choose the periwinkle blue batik with design stitched in gold thread. Perhaps late in the evening my wife would turn the light higher.

I wonder what astronaut Michael Collins thought as he circled his spacecraft into the darkness of the moon, leaving behind Neil Armstrong and Buzz Aldrin to walk its bright side. The mythical darkness draws me, the dark woods the explorer Dante entered and Robert Frost resisted in "Stopping by Woods on a Snowy Evening." (In many other poems he yielded to it.)

When young, turning inward is mere curiosity. I tried enticing university students to give it a go. Many were intrigued, but only a few shocked when reading "The Heart of Darkness," (Conrad), "The Death of Ivan Ilych" (Tolstoy), *The Stranger* (Camus), *The Trial* (Kafka). The undergraduates peered into the abyss (My, how fascinating!), wrote their papers (Will six pages be enough?), took their exams (Gotta get a 3.0 or better).

For one course of study in the Adult class at the church I set aside six weeks to examine various topics found in the Psalms. A flick of perversity impelled me to assign these good people one particular topic I labeled "*De Profundis*" (Psalms 11, 22, 61, 71, 130). I wanted them discomfited; no tears or lamentations, but at least unease. Could they take the heaviness of heart, the melancholy, and still affirm life's meaning?

Early Christian Desert Fathers turned inward, stripping away outward concerns irrelevant to the divine-human encounter. They sought the "cloud of unknowing" (the futility of human knowledge) and the "dark night of the soul" in order to know the light revealed which the gospeler John called the *logos* ("In the beginning was the Word").

In William Faulkner's novel *As I Lay Dying*, the family is taking Addie's corpse to the mythical county town of Jefferson for burial. Throughout the week-long ordeal, from day to dark and dark to day, the mule-drawn wagon forever moving seems not to move at all. The family overcomes both flood and fire. The body in its coffin is the constant reality: death and the journey.

The novelist spends only one retrospective chapter on Addie, but it's the book's midpoint, like a spine with its central nervous system. Her interior monologue about *words*: how words are "just a shape to fill a lack"; how Anse, her husband, had "tricked" her by them; how, in her most elegiac language, "words go straight up in a thin line, quick and harmless, and how terribly *doing* [my emphasis] goes along the earth, clinging to it, so after a while the two lines are too far apart for the same person to straddle."

She wonders what words like "sin," "love," "fear" mean to persons who have never sinned or loved or feared. To them, the words are mere shapes "to fill a lack" whose meaning can never be truly known until the real self at its center fills the lack and then, ironically, no longer needs them. At best, they remain only "shabby equipment" (T. S. Eliot) for expressing what can't be spoken even when tongued by fire. What then do words deliver? Only "hints and guesses." The "praying mind" is what matters, not words.

The scene is again Jefferson: the novel, Faulkner's *The Sound and the Fury*; the time, Easter Sunday. The servant Dilsey is trudging home from church, her master's young son, Ben, and her own Frony on either side. They have no clue to what she's just experienced. She had heard the preacher proclaim, "Yes, breddren! What I see? What I see, O sinner? I sees de resurrection en de light; sees de meek Jesus sayin day kilt Me dat ye shall live again; I died dat dem whut sees en believes shall never die." Amid the voices and outstretched arms and hands, Dilsey had sat upright, crying in "the annealment and the blood of the remembered Lamb."

As the three trudged on under the noonday sun, Dilsey made no effort to dry her tears. Embarrassed, Frony scolded, "Whyn't you quit dat, mammy? Wid all dese people lookin." "Never you mind me," she replied, "I seed the beginnin, en now I sees de endin."

Seniors in the church outnumbered the school kids, the x-generation, and the mid-lifers. How does a minister address them all; how shape the Good News to someone just turned twenty and another eighty?

I didn't worry about it. I let the News have its way and the words their life. I kept company with myself. The rendezvous was Wright Park, where thoughts glided in and out as easily as swans on the dappled pond. I stroked corrugated bark of elms, soft fibers of Western cedars, mottled alders, hard gray oak. Sensations took priority over books, even though I often carried something small enough to fit into my pocket: Pascal's *Pensées* or Florida Scott Maxwell's *The Measure of My Days*. I joined her in saying, "My dear, dear days."

Another place was my church study, not the official Minister's office with its dark-stained desk and leather-cornered blotter, padded chair on rollers, telephone, file cabinets, brown leather couch, floor lamp with rose-colored shade, and coffee table holding national church publications displayed in regimented layers. Stale smells from the previous minister's pipe tobacco saturated the drapes and carpet. The secretary's office known as the CCC (Church Control Center) was an open door away.

After the day's flurry subsided, I retreated up an ill-lighted stairway people rarely noticed and never ascended. (In case of urgent business the secretary shouted summons or more often climbed the fifteen steps and knocked. She didn't mind.) I kept the walls of my "cell" sparse so as not to tighten the room's already compact size. A single window opened to rooftop gables and tiles. On one wall I taped Georges Rouault's stark "Head of Christ." On another I thumb-tacked a photograph of St. Mary's College, stronghold of Scotland's Presbyterianism and a dominant presence of the University of St. Andrews. A year's residence had left indelible memories, which the photo reinforced. (For the same reason I had tacked the picture to my earlier University of Washington office.) Atop a modest, three-shelved bookcase with glass doors I leaned a rectangular icon of St. John Chrysostom given me by a Greek Orthodox friend. A worn but warm Bokhara hid an outrageous pumpkin-orange carpet an earlier occupant probably considered lovely. On the outside of the door I fastened a placard no bigger than a business envelope—*Gratia Agimus Tibi Domine*—a gift from the church custodian/engineer, motherless as a child and reared by St. Louis nuns.

In my monkish upper room I wrote my prayers and sermons. I preferred restraint to overkill, understatement to frontal attack, cello to trumpet. A personal voice need not dwell on personality nor intimacy elicit confession. Words can quicken without bludgeoning. A magnifying glass turns sunlight to fire. Even silence can be deafening.

Each Wednesday prior to the noontime prayer and meditation service in the Little Chapel I established a routine. First, I unlocked the ponderous church door hinged with iron and studded up the center, right to left, and switched on the outside porch light. Next, in the downstairs kitchen I assembled a tray crowded with a stack of paper cups, steaming pots of coffee and hot water, and two electric warming plates. Going upstairs I took one careful step at a time. I arranged things on the library table and plugged in the plates. The new carpet, fresh paint, and walls heavy with books created a comforting ambience.

I hurried to the secretary's office for the folded bulletins. Her competence always assured me they'd be ready. On their covers was a printed sketch of the tired old building along with the church's mission statement: "With open-minded witness to God's spirit, we seek to nurture the hopes and relieve the hurts of those around us, reflecting Christ's love in word and action." On the first inside page appeared the text for the meditation, usually a scriptural passage, otherwise religious poetry or prose. On the other inside page was the order of service: Welcome, Sharing Concerns, Invocation, Meditation, Silent Prayer, Pastoral Prayer, Benediction; on the back page, the names of church members convalescing, hurting, grieving. I placed the bulletins along six shortened Chapel pews, lighted the two candles standing tall on the Communion table, and centered the taller burnished cross exactly between the tips of flame. I returned to the library to scan my notes and prayer. Footsteps crossed the narthex. At straight-up noon I joined the silent few, sitting with them a moment before stepping to the front with welcoming words. Sometimes only five or six persons attended, other times twelve to fifteen.

When I first started these half-hour services, the gathered souls grew restless if the silence extended more than a minute or two. But they became accustomed to this new kind of time and the Silent Prayers. Alone, each person felt together with the others, one and all with God's spirit. It was a time of letting go, taking in, filling up.

Surrendering myself did not happen at once and sometimes not at all. My wristwatch claimed too much attention or the noises outside. Such distraction was nothing new. The great seventeenth-century English poet and preacher, John Donne, was no less annoyed: "I neglect God and His angels for the noise of a fly, for the rattling of a coach, for the whining of a door . . . a memory of yesterday's pleasures, a fear of tomorrow's dangers, a straw under my knee, a noise in mine ear, a light in mine eyes, an anything, a nothing, a fancy, a chimera in my brain [to] trouble me in my prayer."

I stirred, then stood, allowing a moment for the others to return from where they'd been. Slowly I read the Pastoral Prayer, pausing after each sentence to recall the silence my words had broken. We joined in the Lord's Prayer, spoken in the name of Jesus Christ. After the Benediction we trickled into the adjacent library for coffee and tea. Some left to answer workaday schedules and appointments. Those who lingered shared thoughts about the meditation or whatever pressed upon their lives. After the last person departed, I blew out the candles in the Little Chapel, returned the tray to the kitchen, and put things away until next Wednesday.

Occasionally, I lunched with the pastor of the Lutheran church down the street. We exchanged news about our respective congregations and talked books. Young and earnest, he prayed before biting into his burger and french fries.

One day over our second cup of coffee he mentioned having read *The Way of the Pilgrim*. Being curious about "that little book" Zooey carries with her in J. D. Salinger's *Franny and Zooey*, I had bought a copy for myself. It's an anonymous account of a Russian Christian who walks from monastery to monastery, journeying through central Russia and Western Siberia on his way to Jerusalem. In his knapsack he carries dry bread and a Bible. He limps and has a withered hand. What energizes this solitary pilgrim is a passage from Paul's Letter to the Thessalonians: "Rejoice always, pray without ceasing, give thanks in all circumstances." Somewhere out on the vast and empty plateau he disappears and his account breaks off. The time is in the 1860s. In 1884 the manuscript turns up in a monastery on Mt. Athos, the ancient Holy Mountain rising from the southern end of a rocky peninsula reaching out into the blue Aegean Sea.

It's a jewel of a book, no more than a hundred pages. What my friend and I mulled over was the so-called "Jesus Prayer," taught the pilgrim by a monastery teacher for whom Paul's injunction to the Thessalonians meant everything. The pilgrim learns to breathe the prayer, inhaling "Lord Jesus Christ," then exhaling "have mercy on me, a sinner." Continuing on his simple way, he repeats the prayer a hundred times a day, a thousand times, two thousand, six thousand in two days, then without count or limit. He becomes the prayer, taking it into himself. He lives the prayer.

This strange book evokes memories of half a century ago when I visited several of the twenty monasteries edging both the eastern and western sides of the narrow thirty-mile Mt. Athos peninsula in northern Greece. Cobbled trails connected most of the holy settlements, some of them like the Great Lavra, Vatopedi, and Iviron a thousand years old, holding treasured manuscripts and Bibles encrusted with rubies.

I went in the springtime (of my life). The ancient trails wound up and down past olive trees, terraced vineyards, wild forsaken acres and scrub. Day after day the sky was crystalline blue and the sea shining from shook foil (as the poet G. M. Hopkins said). Each night I slept at a different monastery. The monks shared their evening meal of bread, goat cheese, olives, wine, sometimes fried fish, and for dessert halvah. Always present was the granite mountain with its marble cone. The Great Lavra monastery and St. Paul's clung to the mountain's cliffs with hermitages scattered on the slopes. Others like Vatopedi and Iviron nestled in harbors or valleys. All were built of stone and had slate or tiled roofs. Cypress and pine scented the hillsides.

And everywhere silence, touched by an occasional sheep bell or a deep-throated bell sounding bearded and black-cassocked monks to prayer. The churches were dark even in daytime. Windows were few, narrow. Tiny flames of oil lamps hanging beside shadowy icons flickered smoky light. Incense seeped into every cranny.

Too tired after a day's hike, I skipped the midnight Office (Matins) but managed to slip into solemn evening Vespers counterparting early morning Lauds, one celebrating the end of light and the other, sunrise. Compline marked the day's final service of peaceful prayers and chant evoking life's end. The monasteries had no electricity. At night I found my way across the courtyards by moonlight and along the cloisters and long hallways by the sparse oil lamps fastened to the silent stone walls.

I was young then, still in my twenties. I had not read Pascal, Dostoevsky, and Kierkegaard, and considered Kafka and Camus oddities associated with a newly-used word, "existentialism." For the inner life, Mt. Athos served as a useful objective correlative. April's sun and sky and sea were the epiphanies. The darker side accommodated itself nicely to this Byzantine world of silence and solitude, chanting and praying. Springtime in Greece was my Eden and Orthodox candles and incense my nighttime mysteries.

I belonged to a comforting, peaceful, ordered world. What could be more blessed than praying monks striving to be living icons? I knew nothing about the "Jesus Prayer."

Were I to return to Mt. Athos now, sixty years after, I wonder how I would respond to this cenobic life. Its informing image would not be paradise but paradox, the complexity of history, a fallen world poisoned by hubris and war. Orthodoxy would seem too rigid, confining, its vision of an ordered past (paradise) and re-ordered future (spiritual perfection) lacking present ambiguities. Shadowings would play across the mountainside.

Later years brought other experiences and today's memories: visiting Omaha beach and the white crosses that seasons never alter. Sundays now include *that* Sunday afternoon at Dachau when I stood beneath the ceiling nozzles and walked the row of ovens. During the intervening years I have read the Existentialists extending back to Job and Jeremiah.

∼

What makes theological language vital? As never before, my time at the church forced the question. How can words like "grace," "repentance," "sin," "salvation" become alive? Do social science and linguistics help tell about religious courage, caring, discipleship? Moreover, do we know the will of God? Appalling things happen when people claim such knowledge. Can we presume to know Pascal's Hidden God, Karl Barth's Wholly Other, Rudolf Otto's *Mysterium tremendum*? Does such a God take notice of our pieties?

Questions abound. The challenge is not to answer but assimilate them into faith tested by experience. Words, especially theological ones, are honest only when earned.

Prayer is as primal as poetry, music, dance. Prayer-words in *The Book of Common Prayer* are exquisite. Prayer is the language of religion, the very word having to do with "re-ligature" (Latin: *ligare*: to bind). Prayer connects. It is not monologue, wishful-thinking, self-projection, but the language of I-Thou.

Jesus begins his prayers: "Our Father who art in heaven"; "Father, I thank thee"; "Abba, Father, all things are possible to thee"; "Father, forgive them"; "My God, my God, why hast thou forsaken me?"; "Father, into thy hands I commit my spirit." For connection, God is the *sine qua non*, without whom nothing. Jesus prayed at his baptism. He prayed all night before choosing his disciples. He prayed on the Mount of Temptation, in the Garden of Gethsemane, and on the Cross. Prayer is God-talk.

Prayers spoken by other people cannot substitute for one's own. A church member remarked, "I don't pray. That's what I pay the minister to do." But the self is no less essential than God. The more the self, the more of God. Danger threatens when, for example, liturgical prayers become empty habit or serve merely to satisfy decorum, say, before we lift a fork or start a meeting. The writer Kathleen Norris warns that the "idolatry of words [i.e., prayer-words]" leads to glibness that renders the expression "God is love" no more heartfelt than "Eat your Wheaties."

Public impromptu prayers make me nervous. That I am getting "better" at praying suggests perfunctoriness. I try to foresee occasions when I'll be asked "to say the blessing." I need time to put thoughts and feelings into honest words. I once admired persons "good" at praying, skillful with images and cadences. I wasn't suspicious back then.

The most common prayers are those of *supplication:* "heal me," "comfort me," "protect me," or *intercessory* prayers asking these things in behalf of others. Other prayers are equally important: *affirmation* ("Our Father who art in heaven"—Jesus); *thanksgiving* ("i thank You God for most this amazing day"—e.e. cummings); *surrender* ("yes"—Dag Hammarskjøld).

In the silence beyond as well as between words the spirit becomes its own language, issuing from between the tick-tock of the clock, indeed a roar beyond silence itself.

I often think the Quakers have it right. Words are secondary, the Spirit and its presence count the most. The preacher doesn't preach; his words are no more authoritative than those spoken by others in the assembly who, when moved by the one and same Spirit, tell their own gospel story. By contrast, my tradition places supreme importance upon scripture, sacrament, and sermon. For all their inadequacy, words matter sometimes to the point that the preacher considers *his* sermonic words the highest. The consequence is loneliness, the sense that for all his pulpit eloquence and sincerity the congregation just "didn't get it," certainly not if his words stretched ("yawn") beyond fifteen minutes. Yes, for all his pastoral responsibilities, writing a sermon in his study can be a lonely time and so also driving home afterward.

The Beatles make the point:

> Father McKenzie, writing the words of a sermon that no one will hear. . . . No one comes near. . . . Look at him working, darning his socks . . . in the night when there's

> nobody there.... What does he care?.... All the lonely people.... Where do they all come from?.... All the lonely people.... Where do they all belong?

Finally, again, the words. In *An Essay Concerning Human Understanding* the eighteenth-century philosopher John Locke argued that words are "external" signs for "invisible subjects," that words have no inherent connection with ideas; that words are merely arbitrary signs or marks imposed upon ideas for the sake of social needs. In short, the utility of words exists only as far as their significance receives people's common acceptance. Locke's analysis gets complicated, but his main point is that words can signify what the writer need never to have experienced. Children and grown-ups, the ignorant and the wise can speak words "no otherwise than parrots do, only because they have learned them, and have been accustomed to those sounds." Words are only words, useful to be sure, even if separate from private feelings and revelations—like husks without seeds. Indeed scientific language abjures personality.

What's missing is the union of word and user, each owning the other as in poetic wedlock otherwise called image, metaphor, symbol, or myth. The marriage itself is a new reality, imaginative to be sure, but no less real given the truth that imagination can be a way of knowing. Poetic words can themselves be empowered by a prior source. As for Holy Scripture, it is not its codified literal inerrancy that energizes the reader but its pentecostal fire (the symbol).

Granted the Bible consists of various "kinds" of words: law, narrative, genealogy, drama, wisdom, poetry, each requiring its discrete response. But at its most elevated, its poetry becomes holy, i.e., anagogical (from Greek, *anagoge*, "to lead"), words that lead to mystical or spiritual meanings.

Examples permeate biblical language: the prophets, the psalmists, the gospelers, Paul's epistles, the Book of Revelation—also history's mighty preachers like England's John Donne and America's Jonathan Edwards, whose sermon "Heaven Is a World of Love" soars into sky-high anagogy. The following quotation from this sermon illustrates not only his powerful rhetoric but his beatific vision: "a garden of love, the Paradise of God," replete with the divine images of sun, garden, light, spring, fruit, flowers, fountain, river, ocean, music.

> What joy may we conclude springs up in the hearts of the saints after they have passed their wearisome pilgrimage to be brought to such a paradise? Here is joy unspeakable indeed; here is humble, holy, divine joy in its perfection. Love is a sweet principle, especially divine love. It is a spring of sweetness. But here the spring shall become a river, and an ocean. All shall stand about the God of glory, thee fountain of love, as it were opening their bosoms to be filled with those effusions of love which are poured from thence, as the flowers on the earth in a pleasant spring day open their bosoms to the sun to be filled with his warmth and light and to flourish in beauty and fragrancy by his rays. Every saint is as a flower in the garden of God, and holy love is the fragrancy and sweet odor which they all send forth, and with which they fill that paradise. Every saint there is as a note in a concert of music which sweetly harmonizes with every other note, and altogether employed wholly in praising God and the Lamb; and so all helping one another to their utmost to express their love of the whole society to the glorious Father and Head of it, and [to pour back] love into the fountain of love, whence they are supplied and filled with love and with glory. And thus they will live and thus will they reign in love, and in that godlike joy which is the blessed fruit of it, such as eye hath not seen, nor ear heard, nor hath ever entered into the heart of any in this world to conceive. And thus they will live and reign forever and ever.

3

Home

SEPTEMBER FINDS families returning to their routines. Back from summer Elderhostels and Alaskan cruises seniors again scan the pages of AARP magazines revealing the secrets of staying young. Shadows lengthen across my front lawn. At Wright Park the leaves flame red and yellow, and a southwest wind chills the air. September replaces May as my favorite month.

At church we designated a mid-September Sunday as "Homecoming." Children meet their friends again and even oldsters appear rejuvenated in their hopes for something new. September at the university had meant new colleagues, students, classes. A new church year found me no less exhilarated, prepared to handle whatever lay ahead.

Home, said Robert Frost, is where "they" have to take you in. Throughout his life he sought a place where ties ("silken threads") of love held his world together. Home was the "clearing," the kind a poem makes, a "stay" against confusion and darkness always threatening.

We say we own a home. The better truth, if we are blessed, is that a home owns us, not in mortgage but in nurture. Home is not property but placement, a center where things that matter happen, a clarity and convergence of place and spirit. Home satisfies primal needs including connection with a Spirit to whom we pray.

One octogenarian said one Sunday as we stood in the church narthex looking down the center aisle, "It's here I was baptized. I've been married here twice. Here my children were baptized and three were married. It's here I attended memorial services for a husband, mother, brother, and grandmother." She added. "This church is home."

Home is a healing place. Dis-placement breeds dis-ease. In her aptly titled book *Kitchen Table Wisdom* physician and psychotherapist Rachel Naomi Remen tells true-life stories about healing that have little to do with surgeons, internists, and oncologists. For renewal our souls' "woundedness" needs the power inherent in the simplest human relationships: "the strength of a touch, the blessing of forgiveness, the grace of someone else taking you just as you are and finding in you an unsuspected goodness." "Expertise cures," Remen says, "but wounded people can best be healed by other wounded people." The healer's art is compassion.

The church is the soul's home, a place of further union, deeper communion. Its silence inside makes the outside tolling bell and autumn's distant foghorn more audible and the healing more urgent. "'Tis grace [amazing grace]," says John Newton's hymn, "will lead me *home*." One old-timer told me that the tune gave him goose bumps.

American Congregational roots go back to the Compact written by William Bradford and signed by devout pilgrims while aboard the *Mayflower* riding anchor off Cape Cod on a bleak November 11, 1620. In his *History* he defines the group as a "gathered" community that survived because it had been bonded together in Christian faith and mutual compassion. The more eloquent voice belonged to John Winthrop who, ten years later aboard the flagship *Arabella*, in the middle of the Atlantic Ocean, delivered a lay sermon titled "A Model of Christian Charity." He envisioned Boston as a place where people would be knitted together as one. To this end, he said,

> We must entertain each other in brotherly affection; we must be willing to abridge ourselves of our superfluities for the supply of others' necessities; we must uphold a familiar commerce together in all meekness, gentleness, patience, and liberality. We must delight in each other, make others' condition our own, rejoice together, mourn together, labor and suffer together, always having before our eyes our commission and community in the work, our community as members of the same body. . . . For we must consider that we shall be as a city upon a hill, the eyes of all people are upon us.

In its social outreach the Tacoma church took part in the local Phoenix Housing Network, which provides meals and overnight shelter to homeless families. One week every three months we hosted these "guests." Each time, my wife Carolyn volunteered to cook and serve one evening meal. I ate with the families to better understand their circumstances. On one occasion I sat with Rick and his two small children whose mother had promised to return from Florida but never did. Rick's veterans disability pension failed to cover rent and food.

He told me about his wounds: a shattered knee, a broken hip, a nearly useless shoulder. A spray of bullets had struck him moments after three buddies had been killed. It was night in Grenada (President Reagan's war). After he had been hit he spun around, his rifle flying out of his hands. He lay flat in the tall grass, clutching his loaded service revolver in case the two Nicaraguan soldiers found him. Despite the dark he could see them creeping nearer. He killed them at close range, bullets through the heart of one and the head of the other. He said he re-lives the horror every night and the guilt continues to overwhelm him. I reached across the table to hold his quivering hand. Looking straight into his eyes, I silently prayed that my compassion for this homeless man might comfort and help him. Desperately, he clutched my hand.

To love one's neighbor, whether friend or stranger, is not merely good therapy but the fundamental law of human existence. It informs Jesus' commandment—"that you love one another as I have loved you"—spoken to his disciples in the Upper Room a few hours before Judas betrayed him.

After the death of a church member who belonged to a Northwest Indian tribe, her son made a small cedar box on which he carved a cross and the tribal figure of a raven. At the graveside service held on a windy hillside of the Indian burial ground situated between Tacoma and Puyallup, two workmen wearing jeans and heavy shoes gently placed the box containing her ashes into the tiny grave. One of the men slowly shoveled moist soil over it, then crouched to seal the fresh mound with small stones. After the final prayer, as family and friends began to move away, a bird-call sent my eyes upward. A raven had swooped overhead and was now spiraling into the late afternoon sun. What I saw in its beak may have been a mere twig, but from where I stood it looked like a latch key to a different home.

Whether we define "home" as external or deeply within oneself, the way to it may become a battle. Capitulating to opiates is one way to avoid it. Such was the temptation Odysseus confronted on his perilous return from Troy. As described in Homer's *Odyssey*, he knew the consequences if his crew went ashore where the lotus-eaters lived:

> Any crewman who ate the lotus, the honey-sweet fruit,
> lost all desire to send a message back, much less return,
> their only wish to linger there with the Lotus-eaters,
> grazing on lotus, all memory of the journey home dissolved forever. (Robert Fagles' translation)

To repeat, getting home is not easy. From the beginning, violence permeates biblical stories, starting with Cain and growing ever more horrific with the Ten Plagues, the Red Sea crossing, the forty years in the wilderness, and Joshua's armies. And the years roll on.

Tricked by the Wise Men in his search for the baby Jesus, Herod ordered all male children two years old or younger in Bethlehem and the surrounding hillsides to be killed. At the end, soldiers drove thorns into Jesus' head, nails into his hands and feet, and a spear into his side. Had he stayed alive a few minutes longer, soldiers would have broken his legs as they did those of the two men crucified close by. Violence darkens the Book of Acts—for example, the stoning of Stephen and the many tortures Paul and Silas suffered: "They [the Philippians] joined in attacking them; and the magistrates tore the garments off them and gave orders to beat them with rods. And when they had inflicted many blows upon them, they threw them into prison."

John Foxe's classic *The Book of Martyrs* (1563) records what the disciples and their followers endured. Blood smears Christian history from the beginning to the present.

Congregational Puritans fought the Indians, but in a different kind of war they fought themselves, smitten within by the dilemma of their own identity: humility versus personal assertion, the "I" in counter-gesture with itself. Finding the safe harbor of integrated selfhood was a Self Civil War, which Puritan George Goodwin called "Auto-Machia":

> I sing my SELF; my *Civil Warrs* within;
> The *Victories* I howrely lose and win;
> The dayly Duel, the continuall Strife,
> The *Warr* that ends not, till I end my life.
> And yet, not Mine alone, not onely Mine
> But ever-One's that under th' honor'd Signe
> Of Christ his Standard, shal his Name enroule,
> With holy Vowes of Body and of Soule.

I decided one Saturday morning to walk the labyrinth. Inked on canvas, the entire design covered the floor of the social hall at the neighboring Episcopal church. Originating in antiquity, the most famous labyrinth patterns the stone floor of Chartres Cathedral. It symbolizes life's spiritual journey, not as a maze with its puzzling choices and dead ends but an inward way that, once begun, takes the traveler to his destined end.

In the darkness each candle created its own nimbus. CD voices of monks chanting celestial echoes transformed this social annex where kids shoot baskets and wedding couples slice cake.

I removed my shoes and stepped forth, cautious as a child on Halloween. My eyes fixed the narrow path. For an instant I glanced to the center where a humped overcoat heaved with sobs while I circled round and round, ever closer to the center. The cry was universal. Stepping into this central space—the other person having exited and disappeared—I sat cross-legged, palms up, letting come what would: tears that did not blind, my own auto-machia unwinding like the Bayeux tapestry—child, man, husband, father, scholar, Christian minister, pilgrim. But for the chanting, silence emptied me and prayers flowed like glossolalia: thank you, God, thank you, you, you, for life and now your presence.

Lightened and enlightened, I resumed the journey, going round and round and out, taking the final turn and exit. I left the labyrinth for pathless woods beyond. Light remained muted, candles watching, echoes sounding from regions of the soul. I found my shoes and closed the cross-beamed door. November washed the winds, chilled the sun, sent leaves to their appointment. I learned my Minotaur must be slain again and still again.

November begins to bite. Scarves come out of closets, gloves too, and woolen coat collars get turned up. The church doorbell rings more often—but let my journal tell.

—Visited by a scruffy, disheveled couple in their early twenties. They had been robbed at gunpoint last night while sleeping in their car parked alongside the Puyallup River. They still have food but no money for gas to get home to Montana. Both sniffled with colds. I gave them fifteen dollars from the Deacons' Fund and walked them to their rusted Ford Escort.

—Talked with Joel before last Sunday's service. He was hurting over his wife's infidelity, she nineteen and he twenty. They had been married in Wright Park six months ago, a hurry-up affair. I didn't ask who officiated. Their witnesses had been two strangers strolling by. Joel told me his wife had promised life-long love because she didn't want to follow the example of her mother who had been married five times. I invited him to stay for the eleven o'clock worship service and to continue our conversation afterward. He said it was his first time inside a church. He stayed for the service but disappeared before we had a chance to talk again.

—A grizzled man and his eight-month pregnant wife, both sniffling with colds and now stranded, rang the bell soon after I arrived this morning. A miserable day, windy and slashing rain. They had spent two nights in their broken-down car parked in a Rest Area along Interstate 5. The State Patrol would not allow them another night. I gave her bus fare to get home to Eugene, Oregon. He said he'd cope with the cracked oil pan and join her later.

—Tom, the injured roofer, dropped in again still hobbling on his ankle-cast. Out of work, he asked to use the church phone to call his mother on her seventieth birthday. She was dying of Lou Gehrig's disease in South Carolina. To give him privacy I stepped outside my office and closed the door. A few minutes later he signaled me to talk to her. She wept most of the time, saying what a good boy Tom was and how much she loved him. She said he was ten when his father died. She had kept the family together teaching school. I told her that Tom is a fine man and would be OK. When leaving, he mentioned needing food. I drove him to the food bank, but he was too exhausted to wait in a block-long line. He'd try again tomorrow. I drove him to his downtown apartment and saw the roaches. We talked about his eleven years of marriage that ended last Christmas Day when he found his wife unfaithful. His two teenage daughters live with her in Chicago. He told me he was a bystander when accidentally shot in the hip during a drugstore holdup in Tucson last April; also about his nine years in the Air Force and his plans now to get admitted to a V.A. hospital to have his ankle re-set. (Note: Tom returned home from the hospital a week later to find his apartment ransacked and its walls sprayed with obscenities.)

I've read how shamans bless a tepee, its center pole extending the world's axis from dark foundations to sun-filled skies. Home was where *down* joined with *up* and in the linkage people lived. Home was holy ground to be trod on lightly, reverently. And then the soldiers came, their uniforms a spattered blue. They rent the walls and broke the poles. Kit Carson joined the desecration. The Navahos forgave him for fighting as a soldier, even for destroying their food, but the one act they never forgave him for was breaking into their homes, then cutting down their beloved peach trees, five thousand peach trees in the Canyon de Chelly.

Home is health, peace, covenant, soul; centeredness and connection; relationship to something cosmic that is not us and not of us and, least of all, not made by us, but something toward which, in our deepest part, we can never feel alien.

We think of place as horizontal, a spot on a map or landscape, "There, that's my place." But a sense of place includes the vertical. To destroy the land that people call home is to violate its verticality and break the hearts of those who live in it. Homelessness is lostness; a condition wherein we find no strength and hear no voices; where we are aliens; a mythless, flat wasteland.

One spring day when daffodils bloomed and bluebells washed the bank beside our long, fern-lined driveway, a battered car wormed up the curve, hesitated, then retreated. Its chrome front was rusted and its headlight socket broken. I thought it out of place, an intrusion. When it backed down, I assumed the driver had realized his mistake.

Later after returning home from errands, I beheld the scene, my sanctuary. The sliding glass door had been smashed open. He had heaved a stone, first raising it above his head like Robert Frost's "old-stone savage armed." The intruder had stolen my typewriter, my high-fidelity record player, and a treasured Chinese phoenix rug.

The thief must have raced away. Descending, he broke a fir branch and spun wild wheels through fern and flowers.

What else but a violation, a brutal penetration inflicted by someone with no roots and no connections, whose life knew nothing sacred and landscape existed only for his pillage.

Cortés crashed through the city gates, burst the water pipes, fought his way into Mexico City's temple, spattered it with the blood of worshipers whom he despoiled and slew. He stood triumphant, the great metropolis shattered and its streets clogged with putrescent corpses.

A seventy-year old clergy friend invited me to join Tacoma's Nightwatch ministry, which he had directed for twenty years. Its "parish" was the city's downtown taverns, jail, and hospital emergency rooms. He was "out" at least twice a week. I went with him monthly, starting at eight and returning to his church office by midnight. A typical night had us visiting four or five taverns, chatting with bartenders (he knew them all) and sitting down with customers, mostly regulars for whom the tavern was their nightly pub. He and I wore jeans, he a clerical collar and I a black turtleneck sweater. On it I studded a diminutive Celtic cross I had purchased on Scotland's Isle of Iona.

One rain-slick night at the Acme Tavern I greeted Lefty whom I'd seen before. He had recently lost his job, someone had smashed his pickup, he couldn't pay his rent so now was homeless. Next to him sat his buddy who, glass empty and stained fingertip signaling for another, slowly turned his stool to show a graveled face, spaniel eyes focusing on nothing.

Down the bar sat a black giant, arms and hands like aging oak and every sip a thankful sigh. "How's life, my friend?" "Happy, my mammy call from New Orleans today, say she's doin' fine, at ninty-one."

Timeless smoke smudged walls, muffled coughs, made halos.

A sooty parka hunched solitary, his tractor hands fidgeting a dead Bud. His small round table was his belittered world.

"How you doing tonight?" I asked.

His terse reply, "Whatcha know?"

"Truth's simple."

"What's that mean?"

"We're talking, that's what."

"Where's your Jesus?" he asked as if to challenge.

"Right here."

A long moment, a pregnant silence, then "Man, I luvya."
"I love you too."

I helped him up to a hug. He eyed my cross no bigger than a dime.

Amid strewn tables and cigarette fog I zigzagged out, hoping something had been found.

Wisdom cautions against fully belonging to a cause, system, institution. When hyphenated, *belonging* (be-longing) offers clues to spiritual growth. Longing is a precious instinct of the soul identifying ultimate priorities. The treasure lying within makes what's outside (institutions, etc.) secondary. Home is being true to one's axis in loving relationship with God and one another. Home confirms a person's real identity. But to repeat, getting there is not easy.

For a month of Sundays the Adult Study class considered the unsettling paradoxes and ironies in Jesus' parables. One meeting was set aside to share parables we ourselves had written. Mine was about a game, a mere game, nothing more.

A PARABLE

A certain young man strove to get to first base. He swung his bat well but struck out, grounded out, flied out. At last he hit a sizzler past the shortstop. Proudly he stood on the bag and gestured modestly to the cheering crowds. Thus his journey had begun.

For a moment he thought himself safe but also knew danger lurked only a step away. The opponents would seize upon any mistake, any failure. A friendly coach nearby warned him of these things. But when he saw his chance to steal, he raced to second with his cap flying. The baseman waited to cut him down. In a blinding slide the two met. Although the overseeing judge ruled our young man "safe," the experience taught him a lesson: head straight for the goal. Winning is what matters.

He was now alone on second base, no coach to offer advice or encouragement. He stood far from home in alien territory. Players positioned all around wanted at him, and he knew that few runners on a journey such as this reached third and even fewer home. Most "die" on base. Despair rose up within him. A moment's carelessness would cost him dearly. If only a friend could help. But the next batter failed, lofting an easy fly to a lean and hungry centerfielder whose dark glasses made him sinister. However, the next batter did a marvelous thing: he sacrificed himself by laying down a bunt. Our man dashed to third.

Again he grew desperate. He was no beginner now. He had aged, and from all the perilous running his bones had begun to ache and his hair turned white. Torn between despair and hope in getting home, he inched his way down the final path, which like the previous ones, was perfectly measured, straight, and narrow. He sensed the opposition moving closer. Well-tuned to the crack of the bat, instinct told him that for this effort he'd have to summon strength he wasn't sure he had. He murmured a prayer and dared another step. The pitcher shot him a mocking glance. The masked and armored catcher crouched low and ready. Our man waited, tight and tense.

The ball sped in and with a crack bounced to the shortstop. Our seasoned pilgrim sprang, his legs a blur and his eyes riveted on the monster blocking home base. Now the violence, the lightning combat, both lost in clouds of dust, flying arms, and feet. Was he "out" or "safe," Doomed or delivered? "Safe" was the mighty call, and from the choirs of angels an anthem filled the sky.

Let those with eyes to see and ears to hear know that after life's dangers, toils, and snares, home is where the heart longs to be.

Home affirms freedom within the boundaries mortality imposes. Connections both horizontal and vertical fix our place. For me, home is a priceless component of paradox. Seemingly surrounded by chaos poisoned by greed and militarism—or by fate, randomness, luck—home is where the center holds; where things don't fall apart; where, like the center pole of a Sioux teepee blessed by the shaman, the pole is transformed into what the anthropologist Mircea Eliade calls the *axis mundi*, a cosmic axis we do not own. It owns us.

I think again of a Beatles' song, "Fool on the Hill," and its tragic image, which I infer as the Cross atop Golgotha. Standing around are "fools" who hate the Fool nailed to the world's redeeming center: "The fool on the hill sees the sun going down. And the eyes in his [thorn-wounded] head, sees the world spinning round."

4

Communion

MORNING SUNSHINE filled the stained glass windows along the south side of the sanctuary. It was the Sunday I served my first Communion after I had been ordained. As I spoke the prayer of consecration an ambulance careened around the corner and raced to the hospital emergency entrance across the street. Its siren drowned my words. Later in the service a deacon spilled a tray of tiny thimbles filled with consecrated grape juice, spoiling the dress of a Samoan woman decked-out in white.

Earlier that morning the deacons had prepared the elements: bread cut the size of sugar cubes and trays holding diminutive plastic vessels of dark red juice. (Mindful that some communicants were recovering alcoholics, we used Welch's product instead of Washington wine.)

When I had finished my homily, deacons distributed the bread and juice, pew after pew. I kept my words simple: first, an invitation to *everyone* to share in the holy sacrament defined as "The outward and visible sign of the invisible presence of God—the love of the Father, the grace of His Son, and fellowship of the Holy Spirit." Next, the prayer of consecration which the siren made impossible to hear. Then I held high my cube of soft white bread (the crusts had been discarded), saying, "Take, eat. Do this in remembrance of and *in oneness with* Jesus Christ." The congregation did so, at least the eating part. Raising the chalice, I intoned, "Take this cup and drink. . . ." The congregation complied, then fitted their thimble cups into receptacles screwed into the back of the pews. Momentarily, I espied the woman wearing the stained dress, now agitated and distracted. A prayer of thanksgiving concluded the service. After the congregational hymn, I pronounced the benediction and slowly strode up the center aisle.

I grew more practiced each time that followed. The Communion service the members seemed to appreciate most, though least attended, took place the evening of Maundy Thursday downstairs in Pilgrim Hall adjacent to the kitchen. Cedric, the church engineer/custodian, had arranged several rectangular tables to form a cross. I sat at the head and the twelve deacons along the outstretched arms. Down both sides of the trunk the communicants took their places. Cedric closed the curtains and dimmed the ceiling lights. The church's tenor sang, "O Sacred Head, Now Wounded." (I always chill when listening to this anguished music from Bach's St. Matthew Passion.)

On the folded bulletin handed to each person when entering, I had explained that the Tenebrae Service (from the Latin for "darkness"), commemorates the shadow spread over the land when the one who called himself "the Light of the World" was crucified. Further, I mentioned that the service invites attention to Jesus' presence with his disciples in the Upper Room when he gave to them a New Commandment or mandate (from the Latin *mandatum*, hence Maundy Thursday) that they "love one another." Also, I suggested that at the conclusion the participants depart silently to signify how the disciples scattered into the darkness after the Supper and the hour of Jesus' agonizing loneliness in the Garden of Gethsemane (contrasting with that other Biblical Garden called Eden)—all this serving as our own appropriate preparation for the coming of Easter Sunday. After the tenor's solo, but before our taking Communion, I offered a brief meditation:

Among several Christian heresies, Gnosticism affirmed that we gain immediate knowledge of spiritual truth through contemplation, whether it be in the silence of a church, a mountain meadow, or a yoga class. The Gnostics replaced the human Jesus with the spiritual Christ. Thus they subverted the Christian doctrines of the Incarnation, the Atonement, and the Crucifixion. However, the Apostles Creed answered the heresy by asserting that Christ was physically born; he suffered under the historical Pontius Pilate, was crucified, was dead, was buried. His flesh was as real as bread, his blood as real as wine.

As the 1656 hymn puts it, "O sacred Head now wounded, with grief and shame weighed down, now scornfully surrounded with thorns, thine only crown."

The gospel story of Holy Week, Passion Week, brings Jesus down from spiritual heights of a summer day, or the majesty of Mount Rainier, to a man tempted, angry, exhausted, afraid, tearful, abandoned, and crucified. The story tells of God revealing himself not as some Gnostic guru possessing secrets, but as a person sharing fully in human feelings and the life of this world. And it's here where love happens, *here* in the shadow of this world's tragic cross, its 6 p.m. nightly news. History bears ample evidence of tragedy. We are mortal, and in our rejecting God's love through Christ we are broken. Deep within our own darkness the candles sometimes seem extinguished. But as Christians, we believe through the grace of our Lord Jesus Christ that the Light still shines. In John's words, "In him was life, and the life was the light of men. The light shines in the darkness, and the darkness has not overcome it."

To journey with Jesus on the dark *way* of the cross is to journey with him in the glory of his resurrection.

> To doubters like Thomas, Jesus said, "I am the *way*, the *truth*, and the *life*." The sequence tells the story.

Following these quiet words I served the Communion. Then followed twelve Gospel readings recounting the Passion week. Each reader, when finished, extinguished the glowing candle placed in front of him or her. By now the ceiling light had been totally darkened and the candles snuffed out—except for the single one before me. We sat in silence concluded by all joining in the Lord's Prayer. Again a time of silence, then my Benediction chosen from the final words of Bach's St. Matthew Passion:

> We sit down in tears
> And call to Thee in the tomb:
> Rest softly, softly rest!
> Rest, ye exhausted limbs,
> Rest softly, rest well.

The congregants departed silently. My wife and I and two or three others stayed to put things away and lock the church door.

I once coaxed undergraduates to set aside literary analysis in order to absorb the power hidden in certain American symbols—for example, the black raven, the white whale, the scarlet letter, the deep woods, the Mississippi River (a "strong brown god"—T. S. Eliot). They had no trouble with facts, but to induce them to feel these symbols and venture where they pointed, recognizing the nature of symbolism itself, was as frustrating as inviting them in the springtime to reclaim the mythical white-laced cherry trees blossoming on the campus.

Secularism has a way of transforming cathedrals into sterile museums, and Eliot's Mississippi River into nothing more than "a conveyor of commerce." Likewise, symbols used by Poe, Melville, Hawthorne, Twain, and Frost are only literary "devices" or quirky imaginings of unstable writers. Perilously, the cross becomes stylized jewelry worn (nicely) with a cashmere turtleneck; Easter, only rainbow eggs and chocolate bunnies; Christmas, Santa Claus and shopping malls; and Communion, Wonder bread and sweetened grape juice.

One Sunday morning a choir member whispered to me as we assembled in the narthex to process down the aisle, "Don't announce next week as Communion Sunday. We'll get a larger turnout if you don't." The week before, this same venerable saint asked me to help move the small but sturdy oak table situated in Mayflower Hall, where the Council holds its monthly meetings. (The table had been used during the week as a prop for Tacoma Little Theater's rehearsals, and now needed to be centered for the Council's moderator. I assumed it had been given to the church long years ago by some well-meaning member now forgotten.) Carved along its side edge were the words, "In Remembrance of Me." To tweak me for his own perverse amusement he asked, "Who is the 'Me'?"

For the spiritually alive the cross points to a reality both terrifying and offensive—equally so, the bread and wine (flesh, blood) and Jesus' words, "Take, eat . . . drink." Even his disciples recoiled when hearing their teacher say, "He who eats my flesh and drinks my blood abides in me, and I in him." "This is a hard saying," they murmured, and many "drew back and no longer went about with him."

I wondered how to instruct, coax, invite the "enlightened" free thinker not only to take the leap of imagination to behold these consecrated elements as symbols, but the leap of faith to believe the Incarnation of His spirit.

Historians question whether the words Jesus spoke in John's gospel chapter 6 pertain to the Eucharist in chapter 13. In the same way they debate the authenticity of his parables. Did Jesus actually say "the last will be first, and the first will be last"; "whoever would save his life will lose it"; that we must "love our enemies"; that we "pluck out" our eye and "cut off" our hand if either causes us to sin. We cringe when Jesus excoriates the temple's money-changers, "You brood of vipers." Or when he announces, "Do not think that I have come to bring peace on earth" but instead the sword, setting "a man against his father, and a daughter against her mother." And his knifing dismissal of those who hesitate: "He who does not take his cross and follow me is not worthy of me." At the same time he warns his would-be disciples that if they do follow him, the world will "hate," "persecute," and seek to "kill" them. Little wonder that Peter, when challenged to acknowledge himself a follower, denied it three times: "I am not." This is the same Peter whom Jesus earlier had called the rock upon which he would build his church.

The sequence of scandals (*skandalon*: Greek for stumbling block) starts with Jesus' birth in a manger rather than a king's palace. Because his parables are paradoxes, his disciples failed to understand them and were startled to hear him say, "I am the bread of life" and "no one comes to the Father but by me." The offenses culminate with his crucifixion, not an execution but a loving sacrifice for the redemption of the same persons who sought to kill him. The apostle Paul had it right in saying to the Corinthians that "Christ crucified [is] a stumbling block to Jews and folly to Greeks." Jesus himself is the offense and so too the paradoxes. I'm in deep water here, but the topic grows more urgent and November winds more threatening.

Søren Kierkegaard is the religious thinker whom I find most challenging. His books bear such forbidding titles as *Fear and Trembling*, *The Sickness Unto Death*, *Either/Or*, *Attack Upon Christendom*, and *Concluding Unscientific Postscript*. The gospel's "offenses" he calls "collisions" where the heavenly kingdom clashes with the world. Like a Greek tragedy, the consequence is foreordained. To his disciples Jesus said, "I send you out as sheep in the midst of wolves."

If only the Annointed One had not been so human, not "wept," not suffered and died, not been both God's incarnation and humanity's. As a "suffering servant" he typifies us. To know him we too must suffer and mourn, carry our cross and be nailed to it. Do we take offense at this? His disciples did and many left. Brave Peter spoke in behalf of those who remained, "We have believed, and have come to know, that you are the Holy one of God." But, to repeat, he denied even knowing Jesus. Another disciple betrayed him. As for the others, they slept while he prayed in his Garden of Suffering. The gospel narrator John could not have made the irony more offensive.

Kierkegaard lived by the hard and offensive truth of the Good News. He established the category of the individual as opposed to the category of the universal. The offense is that the singular person has such a reality that his life concerns God. The offense is that Christianity (not Christendom) places the individual squarely before God rather than in abstract relationship to, say, the Spirit, the Universal Essence, or the First Cause. Again, the offense is the thread-like relationship between a singular person and the all-sovereign God. The offense, Kierkegaard declared in *The Sickness Unto Death*, is not that Christianity is so dark, so severe, but that "it would make of man something so extraordinary that he is unable to get it into his head."

The Christian stands at the intersection of this world and the Kingdom, confronting the inexorable paradox: the offense and the love.

Nearing the end of my teaching career I stopped assigning the writings of Melville and Edwards to undergraduates. I never attempted Kierkegaard except with graduate students. The reasons implied nothing pejorative about the students; by and large they were intelligent and open-minded. Through the years of academic competition their grades had made them winners. Furthermore, it was not their fault that they were young. More to the point, these writers required of their readers a cost to be paid, namely, experience.

As I neared retirement the energy necessary to fill the words flagged. Age hemmed me in. I saw myself as a spent sunflower. In short, I was exhausted.

Christian truth, says Dostoevsky's Ivan Karamazov, is too gargantuan for humans to embrace—the abyss too dark to enter, the sun too bright to face. So how to cope, to hope? Christianity's authority did not mitigate the dreadful singularity I felt when confronting the *mysterium tremendum*. Pondering the Gospels' paradoxes and those of Kierkegaard did not assuage my existential bafflement. One puzzle was especially troublesome: "It is easier," he wrote in *Concluding Unscientific Postscript*, "to become a Christian when not a Christian than to become a Christian when I am one." Does the Church *qua* institution protect one from having to think? Imagine Abraham on his lonely journey to Mt. Moriah when for three days and nights he said nothing to his son, each footstep colliding with God's command to sacrifice Isaac. Culture declared such sacrifice murder. Instead of mollifying fear and trouble, faith intensified them.

The natural person wants things straightforward as a safeguard against contradictions that sneak in and strike hard. For insurance we create our own Good News: Jesus as a baby nestled in his mother's arms, a friend meek and mild, a teacher rivaling Socrates. We censor the narrative, expunge the ambiguities, cancel the Trinity, and hide the Cross. We seek therapeutic spirituality and pray to have God turn stones into bread, establish world peace, and perform miracles exclusively on our behalf. As Dostoevsky's Grand Inquisitor knew, we want a conditional belief. One that is unconditional asks too much of us.

To Melville, Mozart, and a scant few others, wisdom came early. To old men it may not come at all. In Melville's wondrous novel *Moby-Dick* it comes to the little cabin boy Pip who, before being rescued from drowning in mid-ocean, saw deep down the "miser-merman Wisdom" who revealed his "hoarded heaps." The boy beheld "the multitudinous, God-omnipresent coral insects that out of the firmament of waters heaved the colossal orbs. He saw God's foot upon the treadle of the loom and spoke it; and therefore his shipmates called him mad. To man's insanity is heaven's sense." Again the needling paradox.

To Ahab belongs a tragic wisdom that is woe and a woe that is madness made incarnate in this "grand, ungodly, godlike man." As for the narrator, now Melville's voice, the "truest of all books" is Solomon's and the "truest of all men . . . the Man of Sorrows."

Before distributing the Communion elements, I invited everyone to partake, "Do this in remembrance of and *in oneness with* me." Interjecting these three additional words made all the difference. The sacrament is not intended merely to jog one's memory, but to bring the communicant into union with the Crucified One. To sorrow, suffer, and die in oneness with him is the crux of the matter. But the required contemporaneity is the offense. To the old spiritual, "Were you there when they crucified our Lord?" we answer *No*, and wouldn't want to be. Like words, rituals can be empty too.

Jonathan Edwards would have scowled at my invitational "everyone." Should the Communion be restricted to the visible saints, the "elect," who have had a prior religious conversion and professed it? That Edwards argued this way cost him his pulpit. The controversy narrowed to whether the sacrament is a *means* to conversion or a *seal* upon what has already taken place. Edwards insisted upon the latter; his predecessor at Northampton (Massachusetts), Solomon Stoddard, the former.

That Stoddard's influence continued to pervade the congregation was Edwards's constant thorn. From the outset in 1727 the young minister had opposed New England's spreading liberalism and spoke against the very person who, not only for decades had been the most influential minister up and down the Connecticut Valley, but was Edwards's own maternal grandfather. Nevertheless, he yielded nothing, igniting instead the Great Awakening, the most fervent religious revival that the New World had ever seen. By the time it fizzled in the mid-1740s, Edwards had skyrocketed into America's pantheon of religious thinkers, where he remains today.

Eighteenth-century liberalism, translated into political revolution and independence, won the day. Edwards's massive theological writings were no match against the popularity of Benjamin Franklin's *Poor Richard's Almanack* and the 60-word Deist creed lodged in his *Autobiography*. Not to be overlooked was *The Jefferson Bible: The Life and Morals of Jesus of Nazareth*, a collection of snippets our third president cut from the Gospels and arranged chronologically in a blank book which he titled "A Wee Little Book," preserving "beautiful" and "precious" morsels of Jesus' ethics.

In the meantime, dismissed by a council of neighboring Congregational churches, Edwards moved his wife Sarah and their eleven children to Stockbridge in the wilderness of western Massachusetts where he ministered to the Mohawks while continuing to write big books that two hundred years later would confirm his towering reputation.

What spelled dismissal in 1750 was his rejection of that pesky word "everyone." His defense was Paul's statement spoken to the

Corinthians in the middle of the first century. After recounting the special Thursday night when Jesus had fed his disciples the bread and the wine, Paul rendered a frightful warning: that whoever eats the bread and drinks the cup of the Lord "in an unworthy manner" will be guilty of profaning the body and blood of the consecrated meal. The admonishment required parishioners to examine themselves "truly"; if they refused, the Lord would be their judge. For Edwards, the requisite to a complete standing and full communion was nothing less than a prior conversion of the heart. To come to the Lord's table knowing oneself unworthy brought catastrophic results: "For he that eateth and drinketh unworthily, eateth and drinketh *damnation* to himself." (The King James language using the word "damnation" makes the event momentous.)

To assist in the communicant's self-examination was the duty of the minister who, in the end, would have the final say in the person's qualifications. The Northampton congregation grew restless; the number presenting themselves for such judgment diminished. Edwards's effort to explain himself in the powerful sermons that constituted his book *An Humble Inquiry*, written during the summer of 1749, proved impressive, but the church members would have none of it. That later the book was thought a brilliant *tour de force* setting forth the doctrines of conversion, profession, and communion mattered little at the time. That conversion is of the heart where one either loves or hates; that it comes through faith and *that* through grace; that the Christian's duty is to "own" the Covenant of Grace prior to any other covenant (church or state); that the believer's testimony becomes sacramental (being "nigh thee," said Paul, "even in thy mouth, and in thy heart"); finally that Communion is a solemn profession of the two parties (Christ and the communicant) visibly united in the covenant—all this became anachronistic to the American Age of Reason which had had enough of the offensive Calvinist drumbeat.

Edwards preached his "Farewell Sermon" the next summer. To no one's surprise he chose the theme of judgment—the Northampton congregation's upon him, his upon the members, and in a dimension reaching beyond tragedy God's judgment upon all.

When the Search Committee at Tacoma's Congregational church screened applicants for the fulltime minister to succeed me, one steadfast member fisted the air to insist, "What we *don't* want is another Jonathan Edwards." Earlier the Adult Study class had briefly reviewed the religious ideas of this most famous American Congregationalist.

Sitting at the bar of Brown's restaurant in the Hilltop neighborhood populated mostly by African-Americans, I spied over my shoulder the old Puyallup Indian couple, brother and sister, both in their late-70s. They were nearly hidden in cigarette smoke and smothering darkness. In my rounds as Nightwatch chaplain I had spoken to them several weeks earlier and now learned her cancer operation had succeeded, tentatively. Despite the crowded, choking room they had kept their scarves and jackets on. The couple seemed content to hold their glasses of cold beer and sit with friends again. They recognized me. I nudged into a place beside them. She told me about the ordeal and he asked me to pray. Amplified music made praying difficult. Joining hands with them, I thanked God for his healing love.

Close by was the bar waitress, in her early twenties, wearing a tight, low-cut crimson dress with black sash. She wanted to talk to me. I wished the Indian couple well, then sidled through the acrid maze of drinkers. She said she had seen my clerical collar (my black turtleneck sweater) and tiny cross and asked if I were a priest. "No, a minister." She wanted me to hear her confession. I suggested we find a booth in the adjoining restaurant.

She got right to the matter, explaining she was doing everything possible to support herself, an eight-year-old son, and her mother, but they complained that she do more. Her confession: she was angry, very angry and exhausted. She started to cry, "Am I no good?" She hoped to enroll in the local community college, but money for rent and food came first. I assured her she was doing all she could and that God loved her. Tears spilled down her cheeks. She tried to daub them dry. I reached across to hold her cold moist hands. "You are good. I know you are. And God knows too. Do you believe God loves you?" A long hesitation, then, "Yes, with all my heart." Before returning to her customers she asked to talk again. I suggested tomorrow morning at 10 o'clock in my church office a few blocks away.

The doorbell rang exactly on time. I showed her to my office, leaving the door cracked open and instructing the church secretary I wanted no interruption for at least fifteen minutes. The woman—her name was Debbie—asked about Communion. A friend had spoken once about it. I briefly explained what it meant. She wished for it. Quickly, I went to prepare things, taking along the purple satin bag containing my silver paten and chalice. The kitchen refrigerator held leftover bread and juice. Returning, I lighted a candle on the coffee table and closed the window curtain. Candlelight glinted on the silver. I prayed, we prayed; I spoke a word or two, then offered her the bread and took the other piece myself. We ate together. I offered her the chalice. She sipped, I too. We prayed again. And that was that. She grasped both my hands but found few words beyond her tears. I wished her God's blessing. The church door closed behind her.

Key words in Paul's Letter to the Galatians (2:20) highlight the doctrine of salvation: "I have been crucified with Christ; it is no longer I who *live*, but Christ who *lives* in me; and the *life* I now *live* in the flesh I *live* by faith in the Son of God, who loved me and gave himself for me." Paul's mystical union with Christ sustained the apostle's *life*.

∼

Why bother? What more do I want (need) than a loving wife and family?—what more than friends, country, education, career, health, financial comfort, living room view of Mt. Rainier and Puget Sound, Wright Park's trees and swans and grass and roses? I've been blessed. So why trouble myself with the "offense"? Why attend to the sick, bereaved, homeless?

Why keep thinking about it? My wife says she lives for the blessings of today. With wisdom that was oftentimes woe she rests her case. And I rest mine, most of the time. I've traveled far enough to validate the paradoxes inherent in the mystery of Communion. The sacrament is crucial (Latin: *crux, crucis*: cross), for in its life is another.

∼

Late November tides push high. Rain sweeps over the water and makes the lighthouse hard to see.

∼

I urged her to call 911. I said I would meet them at the emergency entrance. Finding the streets around the hospital congested, I left my car in the church parking lot and walked the short distance. It was 9 o'clock on a cold Saturday night. The Medic-One van arrived. Beverly drove up behind it in her red Mustang. Two medical technicians wearing dark blue jackets strapped Andy into a wheel chair. An orderly took him down the hall while his wife stood her place at the reception counter. The man waiting ahead of her held his one hand in the other. Blood had soaked through the towel. Ahead of him a woman clutched her pale, sleeping child. In the far corner of the waiting room an Hispanic family huddled, one child curled into his father's lap and the other nested on the mother's breast. The parents looked straight ahead—stiff, silent, scared. Close beside, an old man rested his trembling arm on his wife's wheel chair. She sat with her leg elevated, exposing a swollen ankle fringed in purple and angry red.

Andy lay on a gurney in one of the examining cubicles, each made private by white curtains suspended from rings sliding on chrome rails above. Beverly said he sometimes went wild: would throw knives and forks, rampage naked, defy her efforts to get him back to bed. His cancer had spread from the prostate to a hideous tumor above his left knee. Medications mixed badly, often leaving him delirious. This had happened tonight. She had called me first and then 911.

I spoke to quiet him, this good friend and church member, but my words were those of a stranger. He thrashed his legs and shoulders, slapping the air as we drew near. Fearing he would roll off, his wife wrestled his wrists as best she could while I flattened his legs by heaving my torso across his hips and thighs. During a momentary lull I streaked down the hall to find assistance, on the way passing a shrunken, hollow-eyed woman stretched on a gurney who at that instant relieved her bowels and lay in filth.

A doctor came to scribble a brief history. He injected what I supposed was Demerol and said the CT-scan people would take him upstairs. After an eternity they arrived. The ordeal had exhausted us. Andy lay subdued but quivering.

It was now eleven by the waiting room clock. An attendant reported that one injection had failed to quiet him. They needed to give three before they admitted him for the night. Beverly had to clarify details about insurance. The task demanded phone calls. She looked drained. I reassured her we could leave soon. At one by the clock they—always the faceless "they"—reported the paper snare resolved, but not until two was he asleep in a hospital room. Through it all, Beverly's hair remained perfectly coiffed and pearl necklace aglow as in a John Singer Sargent painting. As we left, a child's scream shattered the hallway.

She handed me the keys to open her car. We hugged and I watched her steer away. Tired to the bone, I trudged the dark street to my white Honda. In a few hours I would stand in the pulpit again. I drove home listening to a Seattle FM station playing Wagner's Prelude and Liebestod from *Tristan and Isolde*.

After my noontime goodbye three days later, Andy died. I wished we had taken bedside Communion together.

5

Tragedy

FRIENDS HUMOR me about my Scandinavian temperament: repressed, pensive, brooding (they say). I laugh it off. In return, I sympathize they're not Norwegian and therefore can't appreciate an Edvard Munch painting or a coastal fjord—say, the Sognefjord—that narrows and deepens the farther it winds into Norway's steep valleys. In truth, I acknowledge what my wife and others know about me, but I insist that Prozac is not the remedy. I prefer Chopin's Nocturnes to the New York Music Hall Rockettes, and Beethoven's last quartets to his political Ninth Symphony ending with its "Hymn to Joy." I make no apologies for succumbing to Sibelius' tone poem "The Swan of Tuonela" with its sad, swan-like melody given to the solo horn. I allow myself entry into the subterranean worlds of Ibsen's characters. I've written how the Norwegian-American novelist Ole Rølvaag transposed Norway's haunting scenery into the Dakota prairies; I titled my book *Prairies Within: The Tragic Vision of Ole Rølvaag*. I've seen all the Ingmar Bergman movies.

I own a modest CD collection of Hank Williams and Willie Nelson. Their plaintive sadness draws me in. The ache: without it, their love songs would be meringue, their laments marshmallows. "Please don't let me love you," Hank Williams croons, "cuz I know you'll break my heart." In another, "Alone and Forsaken," the roses have faded, frost is at the door, the birds are silent, and somewhere out in the darkness the whippoorwills cry. In still another he hears a train's "lonesome whistle" like a lost memory receding across the flatland. Willie Nelson is less primal but no less melancholy. "Please, mommas," he wails, "don't let your babies grow up to be cowboys." They'll never stay home. They're not easy to love. "You don't understand them." Instead, ironically, make them "doctors and lawyers."

It's not only the Nordic heritage that accounts for my peculiarities. Nor do I attribute them to books which I've spent my adult life studying. However, a necessary caveat: books do make a difference. When students chose to major in English I used to ponder; "You don't know what you're in for." I wanted to warn them, "Now you'll get rid of your innocence. You'll question the stuff you've grown up with—all those untested assumptions about God and history, all those comforting ideals." I wavered whether to introduce them to Nietzsche's diatribes against Christianity and Tolstoy's "The Death of Ivan Ilych"—the story containing the sentence, "Ivan Ilych's life had been most simple and most ordinary and therefore most terrible."

Whether Norman MacLean's *A River Runs Through It* or Hemingway's "Big Two-Hearted River," whether Nathanael West's *Miss Lonelyhearts* or Nathaniel Hawthorne's "Young Goodman Brown," mine fields are everywhere and, when they explode, do irremediable damage to the green pastures of innocence. Dante's admonishment still applies: "Abandon hope all ye who enter here"—that is, who enter the imaginative worlds of the poet's "Inferno" or Picasso's "Guernica" or, with wicked irony, the deceitful world of Disneyland.

The point, of course, is that *events* should be banned, not *books*. Nonetheless, books are dangerous, sometimes igniting both shock and awe.

Church people tend to read the Bible in bits and pieces according to what satisfies their search for peace, reassurance, illusion. We memorize Psalm 23—"The Lord is my shepherd, I shall not want"—but ignore the Psalm preceding it: "My God, my God, why has thou forsaken me.... O my God, I cry by day, but thou dost not answer; and by night, but find no rest." Bluntly put, we expurgate the Bible.

As a teacher of literature I stressed the importance of every word, sentence, chapter, scene, and act; every image and allusion; in some cases every vowel and accent of a line. In the best art each component contributes to the totality. In studying Van Gogh's final paintings we do not hide the black crows hovering over the golden wheat fields. Without the birds everything would be different.

Equally flagrant is an editor's using political correctness to justify tinkering with the text. One egregious example is *The New Century Hymnal* introduced at the 1995 General Synod of the United Church of Christ in Oakland, California. Masculine pronouns referring to Jesus and God are leached out. Never mind what the hymnist actually wrote and the deeply-ingrained affection and respect the words have engendered.

In this hymnal the Christmas carols suffer the greatest violation. In "Angels We Have Heard on High," the third verse "Christ, the Lord, the new-born King" is changed to "God, our world now entering." In "Joy to the World" we're asked to sing "let earth its praises bring" instead of "let earth receive her King." Because "our Lord Emmanuel" in "O Little Town of Bethlehem" identifies Christ with the aristocracy, editors changed "meek souls do receive him" to "where yearning souls long to be whole." In Franz Gruber's 1818 classic "Silent Night," the baby Jesus is no longer the "Son of God" but the "Child of God." In "O Come, All Ye Faithful" the "Word of God" replaces "Word of the Father"; in the refrain each "him" disappears. Regarding this new hymnal, critics have argued that such editorial meddling spawns a new religion kinder to modern sensibilities.

∽

What is the Bible's central theme to which the various parts contribute and make whole? This question lay behind most of the sermons I preached. A Christian existentialist, I offered biblical answers ("Here I stand"—Luther) to soulful questions. My starting point was simply that in human affairs something is wrong that needs to be made right. With myriad variations the unifying pattern in Scripture is the dialectic between separation and reunion, bondage and freedom, justice and mercy, death and transfiguration; hate redeemed by love, empty night skies filled with angelic song, paradise lost and paradise regained, the tragedy and the comedy; the irreconcilable and the reconciler, human and divine, time and eternity, Alpha and Omega.

Granted the difficulties in reading the Bible—the genealogies, the hatred, the violence, the genocide; the protracted lamentations, the puzzling paradoxes, the alien cultures, the mystical imagery and numerology; the language (too arcane), print (too small), pages (too thin)—the unity holds firm.

The main problem is the dialectic itself, which defies reason *and* logic. For example, to explain the relationship between time and eternity leads either to a pantheism in which God and the world are identified as one and the temporal is equated with the eternal; or to a dualism in which, on the one hand, a false supernaturalism emerges, an eternal and spiritual world without content, and on the other hand, a temporal world without meaning or significance unless self-derived.

Such abstractions asphyxiate most church people who are content to tailor the overall biblical narrative to suit their disposition. Hubble cosmology and the double helix suffice or, closer at hand, the daily newspaper and nightly TV. Poets and story tellers lose out to scientists and computer savants, to journalists and celebrities. Picasso's definition of art as deception that

Tragedy 59

enables artists to tell the truth is a conundrum beyond popular interest. Religious paradoxes fare no better.

In the meantime, the Sunday Christian prays for God's grace, but during the other six days remains satisfied that scientific progress and healthy capitalism answer our problems. Accordingly, the Bible is for the specialist: the historian to prove its factuality, the ethicist to advise choices we make, the psychologist to explain emotions, the counselor to assuage our upsets. For the weekend philosopher mulling over Life's Problems while sipping an espresso, pantheism seems a nice option and dualism is also handy. But most tempting is *que será, será*; *carpe diem*. Why get disturbed with Christian dialectic that, while reconciling both the dark and light, also keeps each apart?

I sometimes wondered what members expect when entering the church door. "Fellowship" seemed the answer most often: sharing family news, aches and pains and good things too; also upcoming rummage sales and potluck dinners. All enjoyed the Sunday morning coffee hour after the worship service.

At the monthly Council meetings separate boards (Finance, Trustees, Diaconate, Stewardship) attended to their business and afterward assembled in Mayflower Hall to hear the reports—then discuss, debate, vote, assign committees, and dwell over long-range planning and (always with heated energy) church finances. After two hours, usually about 9 p.m., the tired members wanted to go home, but first a prayer circle and the minister's brief benediction.

The deeper reasons for going inside the church door belong to the members themselves. Presumably, they like the music, want answers, seek rest in the sanctuary's peaceful ambience, listen to Scripture, pray, follow the sermon, think, or count themselves among those who like sheep have gone astray yet hear Jesus' reassurance, "I am the good shepherd." The problem comes when worshipers allow church business to distract them. Mundane concerns about building maintenance and deficit budgets insinuate their importance.

Regarding the Bible itself, I fear the members miss the big picture, namely, the tragic theme coursing through the Old Testament that the New Testament answers. Human history being what it is, ancient tragedy is also today's. It's this biblical account that the following pages review.

Tragedy underlies biblical history. From the beginning, ominous events accepted as benchmarks of a Judeo-Christian anthropology leave us edgy. Adam and Eve, forbidden to eat the fruit of a certain tree because doing so will make them equal with God, find the temptation too enticing to resist. Both eat. Punishment follows, revealing an angry God and the reign of moral law. Their choice (free?) expels them from the Garden of Innocence. Thenceforth, Eve's pains in childbirth will be "greatly" multiplied, and Adam will toil his days amid thorns and thistles. Alas, such is our tragic genesis.

In the next story jealous Cain kills his rival brother Abel. Seeing that the subsequent generations behave no better, God, as if having botched his first effort, decides to try again: "I will blot out man whom I have created from the face of the ground, and beast and creeping things and birds of the air, for I am sorry I have made them." After Noah and his family survive the flood because of God's favor, symbolized by a rainbow as a promise of future grace, Noah gets drunk and sleeps naked in his tent, there to be seen by Ham, the youngest of three sons. For Ham's "offense" the father consigns him to be his brothers' lifetime slave.

Before Abraham makes his appearance, marking the beginning of Hebrew history (Genesis, ch.12), one additional event occurs. Vast migrations of people arriving from the east settle in the land of Shinar (the Tigris-Euphrates basin, now Iraq) where they unite to build a city and a tower "with its top in the heavens." Disdaining such presumptuousness, the Lord not only "confuses" their single language but scatters them "over the face of the earth," alienating them one from another. Clearly a jealous God, he tolerates no challenge to his sovereignty and allows no upstart nation to presume doing whatever it chooses. Once again, moral law rules: the Tower of Babel (*Babel*, meaning "gate of God") figuratively becomes a multiplicity of languages and people, evincing not only the contingencies of both nature and history, but the tragic consequences of human pride.

These three mythical (pre-history) stories adumbrate what lies ahead. One day two men ("angels") enter Sodom. Lot greets them at the city gates and invites them to bed down with his family for the night. But before they have retired, "the men in the city, the men of Sodom, both young and old, all the people to the last man," surround the house and call out to Lot, "'Where are the men who came to you tonight? Bring them out to us, that we may know [have sexual relations with] them." Lot offers his daughters as substitutes, which the crowd rejects. Cognizant of widespread debauchery, the Lord spares no one the next morning, raining "fire and brimstone" on Sodom and Gomorrah as well as on "all the valley, and all the inhabitants of the cities, and what grew on the ground."

From afar, Abraham witnessed the destruction as a lesson for his future nation if it forsakes justice and righteousness: "He looked down on Sodom and Gomorrah and toward all the land of the valley [at the southern end of the Dead Sea], and beheld, and lo, the smoke of the land went up like the smoke of a furnace." As for the fleeing Lot and family, his wife looked back contrary to God's command and was turned into a pillar of salt, whereas Lot and his two daughters found refuge in a cave. Anxious that the holocaust had consumed all the men, the daughters schemed to get their aging father so drunk on wine he would not remember having lain with them during the night. "Thus both daughters of Lot were with child by their father," assuring them progeny, albeit "illegitimate."

Unable to have a son with his barren wife Sarah, Abraham took her Egyptian maid Hagar, who bore him Ishmael. The father was eighty-six. Miraculously fertile at age ninety, Sarah gave birth to the legitimate son Isaac. Although Hagar had long fled Sarah's rage, Ishmael remained in the neighborhood and at age thirteen was circumcised on the same day as was Abraham, now ninety-nine.

According to Old Testament history, largely undocumented in non-biblical sources, approximately seven hundred years separate Abraham and Moses. Stitching together the intervening stories continues the tragic narrative.

Isaac and his wife Rebecca are divided in their love for sons Esau and Jacob. The latter swindles away his brother's birthright and, at his mother's instigation, disguises himself so that her blind husband Isaac, thinking he is blessing Esau, honors the deceitful Jacob. The sons' rivalry turns to hatred.

Another story: Jacob agrees to his uncle Laban's offer that, after doing seven years labor, the young man can have the old man's daughter Rachel. But Laban reneges, giving him her sister Leah and insisting on another seven-year stint before getting the prized Rachel. Jacob again agrees while begetting five sons with Leah, two with her maid Billah, and additional ones with maid Lilpah. Finally Jacob and Rachel have sons Joseph and Benjamin. Of the twelve sons, ten conspire to sell their brother Joseph to wandering Ishmaelites for twenty shekels of silver. In Egypt he becomes successful in several ways, including shaking off his master's wife who repeatedly tries to seduce him.

Still another story—briefly told: Joseph's rise to power in Egypt suffices to persuade the Pharaoh to help the famished Canaanites asking for grain. At first, Joseph keeps his identity hidden while recognizing his brothers standing before him. That he fills their sacks to overflowing is penultimate to the subsequent reunion of all the brothers and their father Jacob.

But that story gives way to one even more dramatic. The Pharaoh's daughter finds infant Moses hidden in a basket woven of bulrushes. She gives his mother money and takes the child as her son. Nothing is known of his upbringing, only that he is a Hebrew who grows up as a man of action, murders an Egyptian who was roughing up an Israelite, and flees to Midian (across the Red Sea) where he marries Zipporah (an Arab), something for which his brother Aaron and sister Miriam will later taunt him as they challenge his leadership in the Exodus.

God speaks from a burning bush commanding Moses to lead his people out of bondage. He demurs. God promises him and his people the land of Canaan up north. "I will give it to you as a possession." He had promised Abraham the same. Moses demands the Pharaoh to "let my people go." Pharaoh answers, NO. To prove authority, God sends ten plagues upon Egypt, the one genocidal; the angel of Death kills the first-born in every Egyptian family but spares the houses of the Hebrews, identified, according to God's instruction, by daubs of lamb's blood they smear on their lintels and doorposts "that you may know [says the Lord] that the Lord makes a distinction between the Egyptians and Israel"—this, a most monumental pronouncement. Once and for all and for centuries to come, the Hebrews establish their separation and exclusion.

The waters of the Red Sea divide and off they go: 600,000 men on foot besides women and children, "free" at last after 430 years in Egypt. Some complain. Led by mutineer Korah, some rebel. God "opens the earth" to swallow them; those who escape get their just desserts from plague and fire—all 14,700 according to the story. Still others who break loose from the Covenant are cut down by the brotherly swords of the Levites: 3000 slaughtered in a single day.

As a boy I was taught that Moses "wandered in the wilderness" for forty years. The Israelites did more than wander. They fought fierce battles—for example, against Amalek and his people. Joshua cut them down, fulfilling God's promise to "blot out the remembrance of Amalek from under heaven." They warred against the Midians, the divine Commander instructing Moses to slay every male, then adding, "Now . . . kill every male among the little ones, and kill every woman who has known man by lying with him. But all the young girls who have not known man by lying with him, keep alive for your [enjoyment]."

After forty years Moses finally arrives at Mt. Nebo where he sees the Promised Land. (When my wife and I stood near Jericho looking across the fertile Jordan valley and seeing Mt. Nebo in the distance across the Dead Sea, shimmering through the heat-haze, we imagined Moses on the opposite side beholding this same valley watered by the Jordan River, a land of milk and honey.) Now Moses stands on the verge of everything he had struggled for. He's a faithful old man. What happens next? God announces that he will not enter the land promised him. Why? Because when Moses and Aaron struck the rock in the desert and water gushed forth to slake the people's thirst, Moses had failed to attribute the miracle to divine intervention. God tantalizes this good man by permitting him to see the Promised Land but not enter it.

Nevertheless, near death, Moses delivers a speech (Deuteronomy 30) in which he admonishes his people to obey God's word. "The word," he says, "is very near you; it is in your mouth and heart, so you can do it. . . . Therefore, choose life." To Moses life means obedience.

God has the final words. They're enough to break Moses' heart and sometimes mine. "You are about to sleep with your fathers." After you die, "this people [the very ones you've led to freedom] will rise and play the harlot after the strange gods of the land, where they go to be among them, and they will forsake me and break my covenant." First, God denies Moses entry into the land; next, God undercuts Moses' confidence in the people he's led. "For when I [the Lord] have brought them into the land flowing with milk and honey, which I swore to give to their fathers, and they have eaten and are full and grown fat, they will turn to other gods and serve them, and despise me and break my covenant."

The story's final view of Moses depicts a solitary man, haunted by ambiguities, making his wary way over the mountain's ridge. Having been obedient throughout the long journey, he is yet denied the prize because of a moment's forgetfulness. Furthermore, he will die alone, not in the land promised him but in Moab, a region inhabited by enemies. The tragedy could not be more definitive.

Thoughts and ruminations: Perhaps Moses represents ancient Israel, described in the Book of Numbers as "a people dwelling alone and not reckoning itself among nations." With certainty, the mystery shrouding his death highlights God's authority. We plead our case, but a sovereign power rules.

That Moses is spared the knowledge of what comes next offers little relief. Yes, Joshua and his armies will conquer Canaan, but the account in the Book of Joshua chills me every time I read it. He not only puts Canaanite men, women, and children to the sword, but kills their gods as well, replacing these gods of nature with Israel's God of history. Thus, down through the centuries God will oversee all we do, intervening whether in judgment or blessing.

Had Moses lived to see it all unfold, had he seen ahead the same three thousand years that we now look back on, he would have surveyed a human history soaked in blood. I call this a tragic view, a tragic history.

It needs saying that at the very end of the Moses story, as he draws his final breath, "his eye was not dim nor was his natural force abated." After all, perhaps his vision was not to be the land of real estate where today walls and missiles guard its national borders, but an inner landscape of the heart where the Holy Spirit reigns.

Soon after my first interim ministry began I organized an Adult Study class, which I sustained through the years including my second stint. Attendance each Sunday morning numbered between fifteen and twenty-five. I invited outsiders to speak—sometimes Jews, Buddhists, Muslims, local professors, avowed atheists, and special friends. Year after year the favorite visitor was a Greek Orthodox cantor who happened to be a PhD in neuro-psychology. Spirit infused his words. Before speaking, he lighted a candle and a stick of incense. The aroma wafting upstairs to the sanctuary lingered into the 11 o'clock worship service.

Our widespread topics centered on religion. Each quarter (fall, winter, spring) I distributed a syllabus and Sunday-by-Sunday outlines. Several regulars thought the class resembled a college course sans examinations. For one ultra-conscientious soul, I fashioned a decorative certificate suitable for framing, declaring "Successful Completion of Religious Studies 101." He hung it among his Rotary Club commendations, Bankers' awards, and golf trophies.

In retrospect I understand why class members thought me sometimes grim and cloudy. What they encountered was a person who recognized both fire and pathos in the biblical narrative—stories of great human nobility and ugly evil, letters both humbling and harsh, poetry both comforting and jarring. They saw me as one who read the Bible not only as Scripture but as a worldwide literary classic depicting collective humanity and individual subjectivity. To them I was a person of thought and feeling who tried to make his energy contagious. When studying the Hebrew narratives, I tilted toward the melancholy Moses, Jeremiah, Job, the Psalmist, and the Preacher in Ecclesiastes—books in which every theme of glory has its tragic opposite.

I insisted upon facing the total text, taking the words the writer wrote while reckoning with the fact that these texts also had had their editors, redactors, translators. I wanted nothing deleted or amended. This was not biblical literalism but textual honesty. I read the stories as telling more than literal history and, in the New Testament, as proclaiming Jesus as more than merely a wise human teacher whose end was the gross darkness of the tomb.

Old Testament books of narrative history loosely equal in number those books of prophecy, as if the judgments of the prophets kept step with historical events. As centuries rolled on and Hebrews finally secured a united kingdom—approximately three hundred years after Moses—prophetic voices sounded tragic antiphon. For example, the prophet Nathan foretold that David and Bathsheba's first-born child would die: "On the seventh day the child died," this after David had connived to have Uriah killed in battle in order to take his wife Bathsheba for himself. Later, David's son Absalom, seeking to seize his father's throne, raised a conspiratorial army, which in one day's battle left twenty thousand men dead. Although defeated, Absalom enjoyed, one supposes, the memory of having "gone into" his father's concubines "in the sight [from rooftops] of all Israel." David's younger son Solomon inherited the kingdom, lusted after gold and women (seven hundred wives and three hundred concubines), and built a magnificent temple. However, corruption permeating the royal family fractured the very kingdom King David had united.

It bears remembering that much earlier the Hebrews' first king had foreseen the consequences. Samuel knew that accepting the kingship would signal the establishment of nationhood itself. He had wanted to name his sons as judges, following the practice of tribal leadership set forth after Joshua had conquered Canaan. In a severe, prophetic lecture (I Sam. 8), Samuel warned the people about "the ways of kings," their earthly power usurping divine authority. In response, the people shouted "No! but we will have a king over us, that we may be like all the nations." They knew neither the price nor the irony. Samuel acceded with the chastening word, "You have this day rejected your God."

Aging Samuel soon saw the second king step forth, Saul, who "does foolishly." He is best remembered for attempting to pin the young lyre-playing David to the wall with a spear. Consumed by madness in fearing that the priests around him were switching allegiance to David, King Saul ordered Doeg, a foreigner loyal to the King, to slay them. Doeg obeyed, eighty-five in one day. At Nob, the "city of the priests," he killed "both men and women, children and sucklings, oxen, asses and sheep." Such are the commands that Kings make; such is tragic history.

Three hundred years earlier, while surveying the scene stretching out before him from Mt. Nebo, Moses envisioned what would happen. After David's demise and then Solomon's, prophets from both regions of the divided kingdom pronounced their excoriations. In the North (Israel or Ephraim) Elijah, Elisha, Amos, Hosea, and First Isaiah condemned the sordidness foretelling tragic consequences. In the South (Judah) Second Isaiah, Micah, and Jeremiah did the same. Exiled in Babylon, Ezekiel collected his warning prophecies. In short, Israel had lasted only some two hundred years before falling to Assyria in 721 BC. About a hundred and forty years later (580 BC) the armies of Babylon finished off both Assyria and Judah. The succession of nineteen kings in Israel and twenty in Judah ended. Jerusalem and its temple lay in ruins. Scattered among the royalty had been other prescient voices: Nahum, Habakkuk, Zephaniah; Joel, Obadiah, Malachi.

The Hebrew prophets were not social scientists satisfied in reducing facts to statistics and projecting future "probabilities."

Tragedy   69

They spoke with authority given them by the Holy Spirit. With passion and eloquence they denounced pride, greed, and folly rampant throughout their land, and they paid the price of rejection or death for doing so.

Church class members soon discovered that my "favorite" prophet was Jeremiah, whom I regarded as the wisest and most tragic. His life spanned the reigns of Judah's final six kings, terrible years of encroaching doom. The people had played the "harlot." (Other prophets had used the same metaphor: Isaiah, Ezekiel, Hosea, Joel, Amos, Micah, Nahum.) Jeremiah wept, "O that my head were waters, and my eyes a fountain of tears." In abject desolation he lamented, "Cursed be the day I was born. . . . Why did I come forth from the womb to see toil and sorrow?" His words joined a veritable chorus bewailing the tragic history.

Jeremiah finds no lasting hope in outward events, no hope in nationhood, none in tradition's religious pieties. However, from his dark center comes a New Covenant fulfilled through love, a prophecy of a new law and kingdom validated not by national territory, kings, flags, and presidents, but by changed hearts of men and women. We see Jeremiah as a gaunt and tragic figure witnessing the collapse of a symbolic Tower of Babel, the edifice of a nation and its trappings of religion. But as in great tragedy, a new truth emerges, revealed half a millennium later on a certain hill called Golgotha.

Jeremiah's narrative ends in total irony. He goes as a refugee to Egypt, the same land from which his distant ancestors had fled. The straggling remnant of Jews (from Judah), instead of joining the others in Babylon, take Jeremiah with them despite his warnings. He feared their return to the nature gods, especially the "queen of heaven," the goddess Ishtar whom the Canaanites called Astarte, the Greeks Aphrodite, and the Romans Venus— and to the same pagan worship they had left behind centuries before. For Jeremiah the course of events must have seemed like a full circle taking him back to where the exodus had begun.

Jeremiah's people returned, fondly remembering that even during their bondage they had had "plenty of food, and prospered, and saw no evil." Mocking steadfast Jeremiah, they now regretted ever having left Egypt and bemoaned the consequences: "Since we left off burning incense to the queen of heaven and pouring out libations to her, we have lacked everything and have been consumed by the sword and by famine." These were the last words Jeremiah heard before he died.

By the Tigris-Euphrates waters of Babylon, a few short miles from today's Baghdad, the captive Jews not only wept but wrote and compiled important parts of what became their holy Scripture (Tanakh), canonized at the Council of Jamnia about 90 AD. After their fifty-year captivity some Jews had returned to Jerusalem and rebuilt the temple under the watchful eye of the Persian conqueror Cyrus. Ezra and Nehemiah re-established and stiffened the Law of Moses. But for all intents and purposes, the Hebrew nation was no more. After a time the Greeks under Alexander conquered the land, then the Romans under Caesar. Once again the temple tumbled. Nationhood had proved no lasting security, their Promised land taken from them. Jews scattered themselves throughout the broad regions of the Near East and Europe.

Jesus knew the earthly destiny awaiting him. For a final time he turned his face to the holy city on whose Mount stood the re-built temple representing time-bound authority. It had been dedicated back in the days of Ezra and Nehemiah with the sacrificial offering of one hundred bulls, two hundred rams, and four hundred lambs. His lament in Matthew's gospel (ch. 23) echoing Jeremiah's, includes multiple judgments: "Woe to you, scribes and Pharisees, hypocrites. . . . O Jerusalem, Jerusalem, killing the prophets and stoning those who are sent to you. . . . Behold, your house [temple] is forsaken and desolate." A few days earlier Jesus had escaped the Jews' attempt to arrest and stone him. Now in Jerusalem, after his entry had been heralded with palm branches and shouts of Hosanna, he finds his destiny a crown of thorns and a cross, an uncanny analogue to human history itself.

For years I have had fixed to the wall fronting my desk a 3 x 5 card on which I typed words written by Reinhold Niebuhr in *The Irony of American History*:

> Nothing that is worth doing can be achieved in our lifetime; therefore, we must be saved by hope. Nothing which is true or beautiful or good makes complete sense in an immediate context of history; therefore, we must be saved by faith. Nothing we do, however virtuous, can be accomplished alone; therefore we are saved by love

So why the special attention given to the biblical narrative's tragedy? Adult class members correctly pointed out that, according to Judeo-Christian theology, God is part and parcel of this history. Indeed religion answers tragedy, but not before the tragic is seen for what it is.

For these members I did not define *tragic* as the accidents of nature and its victims: for example, the 1775 Lisbon earthquake that killed half the city's population; the mudslide that crushed a Guatemalan chapel and the faithful worshipers within; the avalanche that smothered a climbing party of ten on Mt. Rainier. Nature makes no relational covenant with us. "How tragic" the airplane crash, the tornado, the epidemic. "Slings and arrows of outrageous fortune," said Shakespeare's Hamlet, ". . . the thousand natural shocks that flesh is heir to."

Niebuhr distinguishes between these "natural shocks" and the relational ones involving persons participating in a common humanity. History is the account of people relating to people. The seeds of tragedy take root in this relationship—human beings destroying one another, one man-made bomb in World War II killing or deforming two hundred thousand Japanese in a single mighty blast. In the same war, far on the other side of the world, the Royal Air Force alone dropped a million tons of bombs on enemy territory. Six hundred thousand German civilians fell victim to air raids. By the war's end, seven and a half million people were left homeless in Germany. Four million Jews, gypsies, homosexuals, and disabled people were gassed, hanged, shot; millions more were destroyed throughout the world. And since *that* war, millions more.

In his book *On the Natural History of Destruction*, Professor of European literature W.G. Sebald reports 31.1 cubic meters of rubble for every person in Cologne and 42.6 cubic meters for every citizen of Dresden. But he says in understatement, "We do not grasp what it all meant." Destruction reached apocalyptic proportions during the air raid on Hamburg similar to that of Dresden early on the summer morning of July 28, 1943. The aim of Operation Gomorrah, as it was called, was to "destroy the city and reduce it to ashes." During the weeks following that morning, when thousands of incendiary bombs turned this historic city into a boiling inferno, more than a million refugees, many deranged by the experience, sought safety elsewhere, taking with them whatever bit of treasure they could carry. At one railroad station a suitcase belonging to a half-crazed woman burst open and spilled out the "roasted corpse of a child, shrunk like a mummy," the mother's only relic of the past.

According to Antony Beevor's *Stalingrad: The Fateful Siege: 1941–43*, the Germans in that single extended battle suffered three hundred thousand casualties and the Russians five hundred thousand.

I've stood amid the countless silent crosses marking the green landscape above Omaha Beach; made my way from room to room at Dachau where human beings were undressed, gassed, and incinerated; stood alongside Verdun's mausoleum holding remains of four hundred thousand unknown French and German soldiers, and swept my eyes over intersecting rows of white crosses fanning out to distant horizons, the aftermath of slaughter that lasted three years of World War I.

History is congealed in blood. Author Chris Hedges, in *What Every Person Should Know About War,* begins and ends with chapter headings "War 101" and "After the War." Chapters in between include "Life in War," "Combat," "Imprisonment, Torture and Rape," "Dying." The reader learns that at the beginning of 2003 there were 30 active wars in the world. Iraq became 31. According to Hedges, the world has been "entirely at peace" for only eight percent of its recorded history.

On April 10, 1968, the day after Martin Luther King had "seen the Promised Land," James Earl Ray shot and killed him. Down the millennia, from earliest history, the record of brother killing brother spills its testimony. Whether in its mythological, theocratic, or secular aspects, the story is a tragic one. I realize that in common parlance *tragic* is a slippery, ill-defined word. I count myself among literary professors who have fussed over the definition of tragedy—Greek, Shakespearean, and "modern" (e.g., Ibsen, Chekhov, O'Neill, Beckett, Miller). As for tragic history, what is its governing pattern? Is it providential, one that involves God? History helps us know ourselves, what we have done and can do, but does it reveal anything about God? Biblical history tells that something is wrong and needs fixing. For Augustine, in the fifth century, sin meant "to miss the mark." He argued that only in our transformation can we be saved. And this, the world's salvation, is the working of Providence.

Terms like "salvation" and "providence" open a different dimension of history identified as *Heilsgeschichte*, a German word meaning "salvation history." It emphasizes the primacy of revelation within historical context and the world's subsequent redemption. But still we ask about the tragic trajectory that seems already fixed, sparing persons who live in darkness and destroying the One committed to the light. The irony in John's gospel surpasses the others in delineating the world in which Jesus was born, suffered, and died. People sought his death for healing neighbors on the Sabbath; jeered him for being a common Nazarene; shouted "madman" and demanded he be stoned for his loving kindness. Meanwhile, expeditious and crafty Caiaphas reasoned, "One man should die [be scapegoated] for the people [so that] the whole nation should not perish." The executioners justified their deed as a "service to God."

Despite his teachings, proclamations, and miracles of healing, Jesus failed to identify himself or, more accurately, to be recognized. His disciples followed him early on, then murmured against him, drew back, denied knowing him, and abandoned him.

In tragedy, evil wins over good. Pride, greed, envy, and hate outlast love. Sin triumphs over righteousness, war over peace. Unless enforced, law gives way to lawlessness. New York City requires the equivalent of three army divisions to police itself.

Secular history (social, political, economic, military) gives no credence to *Heilsgeschichte* which records a radically different story, making the tragic, comedic; the weak, strong; the last, first; the humbled, glorified. Time is not measured by clocks but by one's entry into the spirit of light, the same light that shone at the multi-dimensional events of Christmas and Easter—indeed the same light that radiates the glorious *Now*. Partaking of it is to live and breathe.

In the paradox comes the unequivocal Christian promise: "on earth as it is in heaven"; "the Word made flesh and dwelt among us"; "peace on earth, goodwill to men." Salvation history transcends not only linear but cyclical time which, like the morbid wheel of Ixion, recycles itself endlessly as does a clock or a season.

In the narthex of a nearby church hangs the twentieth century's most arresting photograph, taken by an astronaut—the earth a gorgeous blue and white marble sailing alone in the immensity of space. Beneath are stark words printed in bold type: "It's a vicious world, without God." An accompanying photograph is that of the mushroom cloud rising from Hiroshima on August 5, 1945.

In John's gospel Jesus repeatedly addresses the paradox of his living in this world but not being of it. It was this world ("from below") that killed him, the same in which we live, make war, get old, and die. I see again the church door and what's on the other side.

During the final months of James' life in a local nursing home, I fed him lunch each Tuesday and Thursday to give his wife relief. Residents who had been helped into their wheelchairs waited for the dining room doors to open. The hallway was a traffic jam. I pushed him to his assigned table, locked his wheels and tied his bib. Stout aides wearing their ID badges delivered the trays. James was one of five at his table.

The residents (patients) sat like wilted sunflowers, gazing downward at the food or their folded hands—indeed more like dolls withered by storms and seasons, waiting to be fed watery vegetable soup, cheese sandwiches oozing mayonnaise, juice, and dessert: vanilla pudding, jello with a cookie, canned fruit, or a wedge of pie.

James' heavy eyelids canceled nearly all his noonday light. I spooned his soup, urged bread to unresponsive lips, spoke softly how to suck a straw. Cancer, lodged deep within his brain, had left him mute. Across the table Charlotte begged the aide, "Take me to the hairdresser." On other wild days were different supplications ignored of course by heaven's angels. From elsewhere in the vast dining room someone cried, "Help me. Help me."

I wheeled James back to his room and drove away. The autumn maples and poplars seemed to defy death, the riot of yellows and reds distilled by an alchemy already touched by mortality like that of people and nations. And I kept hearing, "Help me, *me*."

6

Age

For most of my life I've lived in the Pacific Northwest, internalizing its landscape and winter rain, seldom stormy, more often a misty scrim. The sun no longer ignites the dying leaves or etches sumi shadows on brick walls. December softens the outlines. From my living room window which frames Tacoma's portion of Puget Sound, the sky-land-water merge into gradations of dark green and gray. Except for its muffled foghorn, the Brown's Point Lighthouse is lost. My wife says the scene reminds her of a Japanese landscape.

In Junichiro Tanizaki's slender book about aesthetics, *In Praise of Shadows*, he describes with special affection dusky lacquered surfaces, light diffused through paper, flickering candlelight. For him a faint glow induces meditation in contrast with shiny surfaces and strong, clean light; he dislikes electric lights and polished silver tableware. He prefers things aged: wood surfaces with dark, smoky patinas—much like the age-old faces I meet when walking daily along the two-mile stretch of waterfront near my home—or when in the pulpit I see mine in those sitting in the pews.

After an uninterrupted morning's work in my church study I often zipped up my parka and took my brown-bag lunch to Wright Park's Senior Center and its twenty-five-cent coffee. Throughout this wintry-shrouded park the venerable trees stood stark and bare: the red oak, the English walnut, the linden, maple, sycamore, beech, elm, chestnut, where months before sweet birds sang.

What also drew me to the Center was the Friday rag-tag assemblage of aging musicians playing tunes of the '30s and '40s. They arranged themselves: saxophones and clarinets in the front row and a trumpet, trombone, snare drum, and bass fiddle in the back, among them arthritic Chester, George bald and obese, Wendell nearly blind. For this weekly dance the ladies wore nice dresses with matching beads and earrings, and yesterday's fashion shoes with heels. Everyone knew the songs and the aching promises of blue skies, moonlit nights, sentimental journeys. Week after week the old Wright Park guys played such favorites as "Peg 'o My Heart," "Maria Elena," "Fascination," "I Can't Begin to Tell you," "Kiss Me Once and Kiss Me Twice," "Seems Like Old Times." I conjured up Dinah Shore, Helen Forrest, Dick Haymes, Bing Crosby, Vaughn Monroe. Magic made Chester's trumpet Harry James's.

A dozen or more oldsters showed up. Whether waltz or fox trot, the common step was an unsteady shuffle emboldened by an occasional random flair. One Friday in early December only eight came, seven women and a man. After getting through a set of three tunes he limped heavily to the open dining room where I sat with my cheese sandwich, orange, and coffee cup. He puffed his way to a table near mine, slumped into a chair, and sighed. In feeble effort to converse I asked, "Too much dancing?" He looked over his shoulder, then turned his face away, covering it with parchment hands. He made no reply, just sat hunched over, elbows on the table, and face hidden. And what about the ladies, several sitting alone, two dancing together? The music-makers had begun again, this time playing the "Anniversary Waltz."

Life is an age-old story that leaves the sojourner sadder but wiser. Mortality is his wisdom, disclosing the gift of life unless he is left wondering what it was all for and whether it really matters since the world forgets anyway. The old-timers at the Senior Center will be replaced by new old-timers who will repeat the pattern. The Park receives its fallen leaves and, as the poet Tennyson's Tithonus intones, "After many a summer dies the swan."

Admittedly, these ruminations are personal yet unavoidable considering my university career committed me to "profess" literature, the best that has been thought and said. In uncertain ways I've matched the tortured footsteps of some great writers whose high art confirms the comedy and the tragedy of life. They've seen the bright side, but have also plumbed where life becomes complex and melancholy.

When Robert Browning penned, "Grow old along with me! / The best is yet to be, / the last of life, for which the first was made," he was eyeing a deeper truth than that of sunshine smiles advertised in senior retirement brochures. Scars of age purchased an even better wisdom in his *Love Among the Ruins* and in his contemporary Matthew Arnold's "Dover Beach": "Ah, love, let us be true/ To one another." For in this world he no longer found "certitude nor peace nor help for pain"—only love, memories, and the miracle of poetry transforming melancholy into beauty. The same may be said about Beethoven's last string quartets or, consummately, Schubert's adagio in his C-major string quintet. Like tasting the best Armagnac, I reserve this music for special times when I really need it, as I do with other treasures: Mozart's *Requiem* with its opening bars begotten of foreknowledge of things to come, Brahms' in *A German Requiem,* and also the heart-rending, throbbing "Crucifixus" in Bach's B-Minor Mass.

Winter suggests something more, the mystic's *via negativa*. The soul enters the dark night in order to know the light. St. John of the Cross, the sixteenth-century Spanish mystic, nurtured his Christian faith on the paradox of dark and light. In contemplation he discovered the truth that "blinds." Paradox informs the anonymous fourteenth-century English mystic's book, *The Cloud of Unknowing*, which describes *via negativa* as the "blankness of ignorance, or cloud of unknowing" out from which God's love is known.

At my age I stop asking certain questions. When younger, I thought such a time would (must) never come. I assured my students that asking questions was the way to grow. Otherwise, answers mean nothing. I played the gadfly, but questions can be a game, a pernicious play, a way of escaping honest acknowledgment that one *doesn't* know.

I say I've stopped questioning, but that's hardly true. Whether on one side of the church door or the other, I continue ruminating as the pages ahead will testify. For example, I return again and again to the Book of Job and its questions swirling around the central one, "Why me?" Impatient with his friends' easy platitudes, Job voices Everyman's complaint: "I cry to thee and thou dost not answer me." Not humbled by God's silence, Job thunders his challenge: "Here is my signature [*my* claim]! Let the Almighty answer!" Out of the theophanous whirlwind God taunts Job for his presumption in demanding answers. Finally, the light of wisdom breaks through. Job confesses his finitude. His questions cease, replaced by repentance for his having demanded the right to understand things "too wonderful" for human eyes and ears to know. Faith quiets the soul, yet we swim the rapids and eddies of life and, as we age, the certainty of death. "We are like grass," the Psalmist said, "which flourishes in the morning, but in the evening "fades and withers" (Psalm 90).

As a child I went with my parents to evangelical camp meetings in Tacoma where, with outstretched arms, itinerant preachers would plead with aging folk to come to the altar and be "saved." "Come, come, tomorrow may be too late." Old folks whom I imagined were mill workers like my uncle Olaf or carpenters like my father would hump over and sob, "Yes, Jesus, yes, yes." I wanted none of it. I dreaded the altar calls. They frightened me, so alien to my young years. I was glad my parents never "went forward." After the praying stopped and we made our way outside the huge tent with its sawdust floor, I raced across the open field, circled and whirled under the stars, and joyously waited for my parents to catch up. To be young was to accept without thought the natural world. "Bliss it was in that dawn to be alive, / But to be young was very Heaven." William Wordsworth had caught childhood perfectly.

Middle years force us out of Eden.

What the apostle Paul calls "spiritual" maturity is to accept life, love it, suffer, and rejoice in it, not as a child but as one acquainted with the night. Maturity presupposes entanglement in life's journey that in the end returns us to the source of our true being. A welcoming Father stands ready to receive his prodigally wayward children. He prepares the feast.

Every first and third Thursday of the month some of the retired men of the church gathered for lunch at Captain Nemo's restaurant, the name taken from Jules Verne's 1870 semi-scientific novel *20,000 Leagues under the Sea*. Unlike the better-attended Women's Fellowship monthly luncheons that worried over important things—treasurer's reports, old business and new, a "meditation," guest speakers, and publicized programs—the old grouches sat and ate, saying little consequential and seldom anything churchy. Sometimes the waitress serving us in our special room inquired, "Why are you guys so quiet today?"

Although as minister I felt duty-bound to attend, I enjoyed the companionship. Sports dominated the agenda that ranged over local politics, cars, gardens, and memories of long ago when kids learned the value of real money, real work, real war.

Age had scoured these men and soured several. They were in their seventies and eighties. One, a retired colonel, was ninety-four. Others: a butcher, tugboat captain, printer, army chaplain, appliance repairman, banker, postal worker, truck driver, sergeant major, high school English teacher (who complained we weren't intellectual enough), grocer, house painter. They may have entered the deep waters within themselves, but rarely gave a hint. Words do not suffice.

I am fortunate to live close to the local university's library. As I roam the stacks I see only an occasional student doing the same. However, if I wish to use one of the forty computers arranged ten to a row I'd have to wait in line, but I rarely bother. Prowling among the 300s and 800s (Library of Congress decimal call numbers loosely designating categories of religion and literature) brings quaint pleasure that extends to a quiet corner or vacant carrel. To hold a book, turn its pages, find friendship with it—such simple delights computers do not give: nothing human, nothing warmly tactile.

Age transforms certain objects into treasure. On my basement work bench I have my father's carpenter tools. I confess sometimes caressing his hammer that drove a million nails, clenching one of his cross-cut saws and eyeing down its ridge of teeth, playing my fingers over his chisels, brace and bits, steel square and awl. No electric saws and drills here, no power screwdrivers, no staple guns. His tools were intimate extensions of himself, instruments of art and craftsmanship. At Christmas and birthdays I've started giving away his tools, one at a time, to each of my three children now in their late forties and over. Perhaps some day they will understand my feelings when they'll give my books to their own dear children.

"To everything there is a season, and time to every purpose under heaven." These words from Ecclesiastes sound worn-out today; modernity has stripped away the mystery of aging and instead prescribes cruises and golf courses and Lawrence Welk.

To questions once spiritual, secularism gives no answers. Pop-culture hardly inspires meditation or gives a second look to lichen-covered churches and Gothic ruins—or to the elderly.

Fact: aging ends in death, the ultimate enigma. As theologian Henri Nouwen and Walter J. Gaffney write in *Aging: The Fulfillment of Life*, "Everyone will age and die, but this knowledge has no inherent direction." An absent polestar brings to full consciousness a sense of dread. Thus again the Psalmist says, "So even to old age and gray hairs, O God, do not forsake me."

My last visit was a September afternoon. She lay on the couch in her living room, the warm and mellow sun slanting through the open front door. A church member, she earlier had been a university student of mine: young, ebullient, eyes bright and full of joy. Now I was her minister. We did not hurry our conversation. Time invited silence.

I said, "Jennifer, we need to listen to voices in flowers and trees; voices in the afternoon sun and shadow; listen to what silence tells us, for in silence we find meanings." Together, her voice and mine, both silent, we spoke of loving friendship.

Softly I asked, "What do you know?" She told of knowing change, knowing growth, knowing love. These were my treasures too.

On her coffee table lay a book of Emily Dickinson's poetry. I asked if she had a favorite. It was page 17. This is what I read to her:

> "Hope" is the thing with feathers—
> That perches in the soul—
> And sings the tune without the words—
> And never stops—at all—
> And sweetest—in the Gale—is heard—
> And sore must be the storm—
> That could abash the little Bird
> That kept so many warm—

> I've heard it in the chillest land—
> And on the strangest Sea—
> Yet, never, in Extremity,
> It asked a crumb—of Me.

She didn't need to speak. She knew its meaning and so did I.

The memory of that afternoon is the voice I still hear, like that of the poet's bird, perhaps a wren, a thrush, sending me its song of love and hope. Nothing is ever finished until the song has done its perfect work.

I sat with Arthur and with death. Death smoothed curtains quieting the room, caressed family pictures, hovered over paper cups and pills, lolled beside the calla lily.

He had built the house, every perfect splice and joint, every cupboard, every length of oak for floor and stair; dug the basement all year long with pick and shovel; anchored the foundation. Driven by love and dream, working all alone, he had started the morning after his wedding night some sixty years ago.

But for the cancer, morphine owned his world. Like a molded lid, his blanket fitted every bulge of bone. Farewells spoken, he lay weightless, waiting—eyes forgotten by the sun, mouth aslant, trickling—waiting Death who kindly sat with me.

I edged my chair to where Oscar lay. Outside, rain glossed green leaves. Inside, morphine dripped drop by drop, invading his wrist blotched by needles of a different kind.

Down the narrowing hallway here in this last room reserved for the dying, the final kisses and strokes of hand, two strangers wearing black would soon be summoned. They would lift him for the gurney ride to the waiting hearse.

He lay comatose. Yet I knew that hearing is the last of our senses to go. Up close, I whispered words from my pocket New Testament: valley of shadows . . . grass that flourishes and withers . . . house of many mansions . . . death swallowed up in victory. The words dissolved into the vision I imagined we now shared: trees forever fruitful . . . crystal river pure.

On the day my father died (his name was Peter) I spooned him jello and waited his last words. It was January 3, 1976. As night darkened the hospital window, he murmured, "The Christmas music this year was beautiful."

Things change in the remembering. What my father was has changed to what he is. It's a sea change born of tears. What we call an end is a beginning. The end is where we start from and know the person as if for the first time.

This is not an easy belief. Nothing paradoxical is easy. Yet if we accept death, if we give up holding to what is irretrievably gone, the nothing that is left is not barren but enormously fruitful. Out of the darkness what we have lost comes beaming back again. Through tears and memory I know my father anew. In his death is new sonship, new love, and the endless possibilities of new meaning.

More ruminations: years before I was ordained, winter in New Haven arrived fast, an early dusting of snow and long, cold nights. One Sunday afternoon I walked down to hear the carillon concert pealing from the Gothic tower rising above Dwight Chapel. The streets were empty except for a few hurrying scarves. Branford Cloister where I chose to listen kept the wind away but not the cold. Wanting the warmth of Dwight across the street, I entered as the west window faded into night and the carillon outside sent forth a final "Rejoice, Rejoice," a carol for this first Sunday of Advent.

The next day snow swept through the Yale Divinity colonnades and drifted against the chapel door. I watched students arranging green garlands and giant red ribbons. There they were, the students, sporting up and down their time-bound ladders, preparing for a birth taking us out of time. It was a difficult birth that cost others born that holy night to be slaughtered by Herod's sword while Mary and Joseph hurried their child away. This day, the Yale students erected a pitch-scented tree symbolizing another paradox: birth and death, tree and cross, nativity and the promise of crucifixion. Only a few days after the birth, Simeon prophesied the other, saying to the mother, "A sword will pierce your soul, too." Birth and the tragedy to come. It was almost Christmas when we left for Scotland. I said goodbye to friends, strolled a final time through the corridors, and peered into the chapel.

What was Christmas Eve like in Edinburgh? Carolyn stayed in, nursing a sprained ankle. I bent into slashing winds from the Firth of Forth to St. Serf's parish church. I had seen a poster announcing Handel's "Messiah." At three o'clock the afternoon light was nearly spent. Inverleith Row was a rain-slicked street with slithery amber splotches reflecting street lights.

Nothing in the church was warm except the several hands that greeted me. A few persons huddled near the front. I sat next to a stone pillar halfway back. Christmas lights hanging limply on a meager spruce daubed the marble pulpit red. Partially hidden, the singers took their places behind the rood screen. Most kept their coats and scarves on. The opening chord sent a chill of recognition. The closing one that ended all the Hallelujahs did the same. I was glad to leave. The singing had been shaky, the baritone perhaps the next-door fishmonger and the soprano a hairdresser. The image of the crib stuffed with straw and holding a plastic doll stayed with me down the watery street. A fine walk, the Christmas Eve, returning from the "Messiah."

∾

Winter in Edinburgh was a passageway through which a trampling wind howled from the east. I explored the streets—first to Stockbridge, on to Moray Place, Charlotte Square, and Palmerston where St. Mary's Cathedral dwarfed surrounding terraces; then to Dean Village, back to Henderson and Rodney Streets, over to Annandale, around behind Calton Hill, through Tolbooth Wynd that passes graves of Adam Smith and Burns's own Clarinda, down to Holyrood, and up to St. Giles with its airy spire. The labyrinthine days included Candlemaker's Row, Grassmarket, Cowgate, Bristo Square, Buccleuch Place.

Every evening I chose alternate ways back from the University: King's Stables or Milne's Close or North Bridge, across Princes Street and down Dundas, Brandon Terrace, across the Water of Leith. Knifing against windblown rain, I met companionate ghosts dispatched by the eastern *haar*. The year ended. Tattered skies hurled past the Castle. Outside my study window, heels struck frozen pavement. George Square became a nethergate. Now was the time to learn that heroes start journeys but mere mortals end them. I went alone through doors that locked behind me. Feelings detached themselves and with delirious urgency pushed down streets and wynds, into closes, halting, whirling among debris, finding still another doorway or iron paling, fusing with it utterly, and becoming the thing past hope of escape or retreat.

Ice encased the city in what newspapers called a nightmare. Blizzards in the Cairngorms had taken five skiers and stranded hundreds more. With all roads in and out of Glasgow, Inverness, Aberdeen, and Edinburgh closed, the country lay paralyzed for three days and nights.

On the third night of the storm I worked late at the University. Engrossed in Jonathan Edwards's distinctions between false and true marks of saving grace, I suddenly recognized the darkness outside. I turned off the gas heater and desk lamp, reached for my scarf, knit cap, gloves, and parka. The icy cobblestones made each footstep a risk. Where High Street becomes Lawnmarket, I stepped back into Milne's Close to gain reprieve from blowing snow. To have gone through the Close was the better way, but tightening my scarf I lurched up to Tolbooth St. John's Church, a dreadful façade, blackened by a hundred years of coal soot. The iron gates were locked for repairs. I expected no shelter but only a closer look, first at the tower and then its spire reaching almost out of sight. Clutching a paling with each hand, I stared straight up the giant spire, slimmer and more lethal the higher it rose, and at its distant tip detected a diminutive cross, the necessary barb. Attached was a rope, the kind mountain climbers use, which billowed down to its knot on a black paling where a sign, crusted in ice, said, "James Clark, Steeplejack." Whoever climbed that rope had to be good.

Modern-day archaeologists say that biblical events, unless scientifically verified, carry little if any credence. Without a piece of Noah's ark, no ark; without non-biblical historical records of Moses, no Moses; without scientific explanation, no flood, no stationary sun, no burning bush, no return of Lazarus from the dead. Historians in their seminars questing for the "real" Jesus of Nazareth seek to authenticate what he said, and, if lacking proof, discount his Seven Last Words, most of his parables, and his virgin birth. In short, without scientific or historical verification, no miracles, no story. On the other hand, literalists claim all biblical events historically true. Being confined by such exactitude obscures the greater trajectory of symbol and myth, and the greater authority of story.

To keep only what accords with laws of nature, facts of history, and so-called common sense stabs the heart out of the Bible. Dismissing Holy Scripture because of its pre-Copernican cosmology and pre-Darwinian creationism, or because historians find no evidence that either Abraham or Moses lived, or because certain stories "just could not have happened" supposedly justifies dismissing biblical authority. This kind of literalism undermines the epics of Homer, Dante, and Milton.

Render unto Copernicus, Newton, Darwin, Einstein what is theirs; render unto the biblical story what is its. The latter requires not only faith in a God whose power exceeds that of nature but also "sanctified imagination" (Jonathan Edwards), a faculty we have by "special grace" enabling us to apprehend what to natural sight is invisible. Such grace enables one to accept the miracles and their countless variations. At my age I no longer doubt the narrative that Jonah spent three days and nights in a whale's belly; that Elijah ascended to heaven in a chariot of fire; that Jesus was born of a virgin; that he healed the sick, restored the dead, fed 5000 with five loaves and two fish, walked on water, rose from the dead, and reappeared to his disciples. Miracles obtain everywhere, even in my own origin and the blessings I've received. The story is the miracle, the mystery, the wonder. It's the angel Gabriel saying to Mary, "For with God nothing will be impossible."

Winter is age's metaphor. Here in Tacoma my interim ministry neared its end. In the sanctuary on Christmas Eve I joined the choir and congregation in singing "Silent Night, Holy Night," the old night made new by love's pure light. Time had been transformed into eternal truth. The heavenly hosts who sang to the Bethlehem shepherds sang to me. My peace was complete until I wondered this winter night who might be huddling in Wright Park needing shelter from the cold darkness.

Situated among the weathered sentinels of red oaks, Wright Park's Seymour Conservatory, which in my childhood I called "the glass house," encloses an arboretum, a veritable world of plants and trees protected by glass-paneled walls and a towering domed ceiling. Outside, cold winter rain beats against the old oak trees. Inside, the soft humidity gives constant comfort to ferns and palms.

Visitors enter as into a miniature paradise, a garden holding two pools hidden within winding pathways. In one pool swim koi, electric orange and white, black and glistening gray. They feed on green vegetation that rims their microcosm and reaches to the bottom. I'm told they sometimes grow to a great age. The other pool embraces wishes little children toss in, bright pennies and nickels that flash their tiny winks. I instructed Maria and John to speak not a word as they made their wish. I sometimes said a prayer before they splashed the coins into the mystical water.

Although heedless of tiny signs identifying the plants, my grandchildren loved this place: American Wonder Lemon, Golden Tree Fern (New Zealand), Spanish Moss, Chinese Lady Palm and Fan Aloe (S. Africa), Strawberry Guava (Brazil), Great Bird of Paradise (Australia), Arabian Coffee Plant, Wattle (S.E. Australia), Mexican Fishtail, Sego Palm (Old World tropics), Malaysia Rhododendron, Crown of Thorns (Madagascar), Fiddle-Leaf Fig (Garden of Eden?).

The Conservatory is a place of wonder and peace, redolent with fragrances of the living world—no cyanide in its water, no radioactive atoms in the gentle currents of air—indeed a garden that hearkens back to where we first lived our wishes until that fateful one changed everything.

After buttoning the children's jackets and my own, I held their hands and left through the east exit. Wind-blown rain struck us at once.

Cracks etch the worn and tired mortar securing the stone walls of Tacoma's old church. Entering through the door quickens me to the creaking floors and the narrow stairways that challenge the aging. Baseboards and moldings bear countless scars. Soon the building will die, and the stories too unless read anew. Serious things took place here: christenings, marriages, services for the dead, Sunday morning Gospel affirmations. Teachers taught and preachers preached, rousing deep longings and a reconciling faith. The center aisle leads down to the Communion table and the Cross.

The ancient prophet Habakkuk heard the temple's stones cry out in rage against the parsimonious hand and heart. The prophet Malachi divined that the temple's moldering foundations will crumble with the news that one day God's judgment will come. "But who," the prophet asks, "can endure" that day.

Ely is a small English town dominated by a large cathedral visible miles away. This "monument to superstition"—as the eighteenth-century historian Edward Gibbon judged the great European medieval cathedrals—stands 537 feet long, 119 feet wide at the main transepts. Its western tower soars 215 feet high. Founded by St. Etheldreda in the year 673, the church served as a house of worship even though the cathedral was not finished until the thirteenth century.

By contrast, today brings visitors *en masse*, arriving in air-conditioned buses equipped with non-glare windows and a WC in back. Clutching their guide books and casually listening to the spiel, they learn a few piddling facts about lecterns and pulpits, fonts, glass and brass, naves, transepts, presbyteries, towers, buttresses, cloisters, side chapels, screenwork—and return to the buses exactly on time. Woe to the laggard who keeps fellow-travelers waiting. After all, the schedule mandates two other cathedrals to visit, time for tea, and more snapshots to take. How else to remember Ely's Octagon—or Lincoln's gorgeous decorative carvings, Salisbury's 400-foot spire, Durham's rock foundation or the Venerable Bede's austere tomb, and Wells's curved and worn staircase?

Other reasons send visitors to the out-of-the-way parish churches which have summarized English village life for hundreds of years. Here the true seeker more likely finds an atmosphere of devotion and worship, sees memorials to persons who lived in the region since Saxon times, and examines the craftsmanship in wood and lovingly wrought stone by unknown villagers to beautify the House of God. What better place for peace and tranquility, antidotes to the madding crowds. I meandered among weather-worn gravestones and knelt to decipher inscribed words almost weathered away by sun and storm.

Such wandering gave me a sense of history's weight and why these ivy-covered walls were set in place. Wasn't their purpose to provide a sanctuary for prayer, meditation, and a different kind of time that crowns life and reveals in history a providential pattern? Such are the gifts reserved for age as T. S. Eliot found in England's Huntingtonshire when exploring Little Gidding's chapel.

As for the heft of history—the tragedy, suffering, hope, corruption, murder, absurdities, search, war, love, contradictions, depravities, sin, and sadness—what solace remains unless for the church's testimony and its proclamation?

7

Grace

For the Wednesday noontime prayer and meditation service I summarized Charles Dickens *A Christmas Carol*. Outside the winter winds swept away the leaves, and the trees stood naked and bereft. Inside the Little Chapel a wind-drift teased the lighted candles on either side of the polished brass cross.

On Christmas Eve Dickens's Ebenezer Scrooge shouted "Humbug!" when his nephew wished him Merry Christmas. The wizened man growled to his clerk Bob Cratchitt that taking tomorrow off would mean he'd report to work that much earlier the next day. Scrooge locked the office, took his "melancholy dinner" as usual at the "melancholy" tavern and trudged home in fog and frost, the night so dark he groped his way to the door. Inside, he double-locked it and felt his way through unlighted halls and chambers to reassure himself all was secure. He sipped some gruel, checked his ledger accounts, and went to his cold bed.

Dickens' imagery depicts a pinched soul locking out the light, but failing to thwart the ghostly visitation of Jacob Marley, seven years dead, who announced to his former partner that he might expect successive visits from three Ghosts: Christmas Past, Present, and Future.

By showing to Scrooge the happy, laughing household of the girl, now a comely woman, whom he might have married had he not chosen to idolize gold, the first unbidden Ghost forced the desolate man to begin the dismal journey into himself. The second Ghost brought him to Cratchitt's dwelling, so wanting in daily comfort but overflowing in love. Appalled when made to realize that even his underpaid employee reveled in human gladness, he begged to learn no more. As education requires, the third Ghost led him to the churchyard where he was told to find a certain neglected grave. There he read in horror *Ebenezer Scrooge*. "Oh, tell me I may sponge away the writing on this stone." In darkness he saw most clearly his loveless, wasted life. My own emotions surfaced when I read Scrooge's final words spoken that agonizing night: "Good Spirit . . . your nature intercedes for me, and pities me. Assure me that I yet may change these shadows you have shown me by an altered life." He prayed that divine grace would reverse his melancholy fate.

Christmas morning opened him to a new world. How to explain it? What but his repentance which Dickens does not let his readers hear; what but God's forgiveness; what but reconciliation? To God no human voice is ever lost.

> He [Scrooge] went to church, and walked about the streets, and watched the people hurrying to and fro, and patted the children on the head, and questioned beggars, and looked down into the kitchens of houses, and up to the windows; and found that everything could yield him pleasure. He had never dreamed that any walk—that anything—could give him so much happiness.

Transformed by divine grace, he joyously greets Cratchitt and promises to assist his struggling family by raising his salary. He joins them in Yuletide's glad reunion.

> Scrooge was better than his word. . . . He became as good a friend, as good a master, and as good a man as the good old City knew, or any other good old city, town, or borough in the good old world.

Scrooge gave little attention to the people laughing at his alteration. "His own heart laughed: and that was quite enough for him."

The church is a sanctuary whether we're alone in its holy silence or worshiping with others. Singer Jessye Norman said to Bill Moyers on one of his television programs that her most beloved stanza in John Newton's hymn "Amazing Grace" begins, "Through many dangers, toils and snares, I have already come" and ends "'tis grace hath brought me safe thus far, and grace will lead me home." Giving thanks is elemental expression: *Deo Gratias* ("Thanks be to God"). Praying expands consciousness of God, transforming the person who surrenders self-guarded "No" or "Maybe" to "Yes"—the acceptance of God's gift of grace.

At the memorial service for a long-time church member, the congregation awaited my opening words of Greeting and Grace. I welcomed the people, spoke briefly about the deceased (I would say more later), named the family members, and prayed that the mystery of death not cloud the truth of God's abiding love. I continued: "Christian faith affirms both life and death—a time for the one and a time for the other. Given life, we're also given death but the assurance of a more triumphant power. In God we live and move and have our being. In God no human soul is lost. In God all is grace."

To say "all is grace" opens a formidable and seemingly intractable puzzle in Christian thought: divine grace vs. free will. Certain questions attest to this dilemma—for example, What is God's will and is his grace sufficient, irresistible? Does God's "prevenient" grace, represented in infant baptism, continue throughout a person's life? Does Adam's fall apply to everyone, but is grace reserved only for the "elect"? Paul's conundrum spoken to the Romans speaks to Christians as well: "I can *will* what is right, but I cannot *do* it. For I do not do the good I want, but the evil I do not want is what I do." He explained to the Galatians that what saved him from this terrifying predicament came not from "man's gospel," not from what he had been taught, "but it came through the revelation of Jesus Christ. . . . [It] had called me through his grace." That event Paul made graphic in his account of what happened to him on the road to Damascus.

The seventeenth-century French mathematician and philosopher Blaise Pascal experienced a similar Pauline dichotomy that no disinterested study of nature and knowledge of external things could reconcile. What happened on the night of November 23, 1654, opened his eyes as if for the first time. After two hours of ecstatic, mystical illumination he knew an operative divine grace transcended whatever natural man structured and claimed to know. (Sewn into his coat and discovered after his death eight years later was his note describing this life-changing event.) Natural light is sufficient to believe in God, he wrote in *Pensées*, but in order truly to be illumined a person must first be "elected" to believe and such belief comes as a gift of faith from a righteous God. Faith precedes understanding (*fides quaerens intellectum*), not the reverse. No one earns a PhD in Faith. It is a favor freely shown to humanity, described in the New Testament as God's grace through the incarnate life and atoning death of his Son. John 3:16 says it best. "For God so loved the world that he gave his only begotten son that whosoever believeth in him would not perish but have everlasting life." Martin Luther called this passage the New Testament in miniature. This is grace, the redemptive activity of divine love.

The memorial service in which I declared "All is grace" celebrated the life and mourned the death of the church's engineer, a black eighty-six-year old. Before and after World War II Owen had been an Alaska fisherman and for nearly twenty years a postal employee. During the post-war years and past eighty, he also cared for the church building as plumber, electrician, and general engineer. In the furnace room his work table told the story: wrenches, screwdrivers, hammers, hack saw, oil cans, WD-40, grinder, vise, assorted nuts and bolts and hinges and fuses and locks and scraps of pipe, hoses, and rolls of this and that.

I liked his "office." It reminded me of my father's in the basement of the house he built, my childhood home. I often perched on one of Owen's stools to discuss the day's news and his own growing up as "colored" man (his term). "It wasn't easy," he said gently. Even the military considered him only worthy to serve as steward (cook) though he'd had one year of pre-engineering at the University of Washington. The postal service was more even-handed.

One day I asked if, as a postal carrier, he ever wondered what was inside a canceled stamped envelope for whom the addressee was unknown and the sender's address was missing. He said he sometimes did, imagining who the sender was, who the intended recipient, and what the message now destined for the dead letter office said. Owen was a thoughtful, sweet-tempered fellow whose deeds spoke louder than his words—not a Melvillian Bartleby, hopeless and weirdly quiet. My friend kept his own counsel and was grateful for the life given him.

Earlier in the year a guest minister conducted the noontime interchurch Thanksgiving service, heavy with holy words. He layered himself in alb, dazzling stole, and what appeared a surplice. From his neck a five-inch brass cross swayed across his mighty paunch. Although neither Roman Catholic, Episcopalian, nor Lutheran, he obviously considered the simple black robe of the Congregationalist insufficient.

Afterward, I stopped by Owen's workroom to chat, finding him kneeling in the darkened corner examining a rusty electrical element he had extracted from the hot water tank. Scattered close by were several wrenches and above his head a single light bulb dangled from an extension cord.

Ah, Owen! Ah, humanity!

After Owen retired, Cedric took the job. A graduate of a Midwestern university, he had tired of teaching art for ten years at a St. Louis high school. Additional years as a social worker didn't help. He drifted to Chicago where life as a church custodian fitted his temperament better. The day he left Chicago the wind blew west. His money ran out in Tacoma where he learned about a certain church needing a replacement for its previous handyman/engineer. Cedric settled in, dividing an unused awkward oblong upstairs room into a three-sectioned living space, rent-free, for himself and cats Carmen and Rosalind.

I talked more theology with him than with anyone else at the church. He was keen on medieval mysticism and monasticism, and gave me a framed delicate sketch of St. Benedict he had done in black ink. Once a week we lunched at the hospital cafeteria across the street, early enough each time to claim the same table in the far corner. Mixed among the scurrying lunch crowd were doctors, nurses, and others still wearing their green scrubs and caps. I wondered what *their* morning had been like.

We talked art too. He favored the German and Scandinavian expressionists who, like Edvard Munch, distorted nature to project inner visions. A stocky fifty-five-year old with bushy black hair and black-framed glasses with thick lenses, Cedric had difficulty hearing. His stentorian voice reached uninvited listeners nearby. Their being privy to his esoterica amused me.

Death had left him motherless at an early age. The strict rule of Catholic nuns who reared and schooled him imprinted Latin, French, and church doctrine on his developing mind. Scholarships and odd jobs saw him through the university. On the same June day that he arrived home for the summer break after his freshman year he found his grandmother dead in the bathtub, a suicide, leaving only his father and uncle as his family. Each had his own cot in the same dingy bedroom of a rundown apartment. Shortly afterward, his uncle died and then his father. He had no siblings, no cousins.

Once, I asked him if he had a favorite poem. He startled me by immediately reciting the octet of Shakespeare's sonnet #29:

> When, in disgrace with Fortune and men's eyes,
> I all alone beweep my outcast state,
> And trouble deaf heaven with my bootless [futile] cries,
> And look upon myself and curse my fate,
> Wishing me like to one more rich in hope,
> Featur'd like him, like him with friends possess'd,
> Desiring this man's art, and that man's scope,
> With what I most enjoy contented least. . . .

Ah, Cedric, Ah, humanity!

Does grace strengthen a person for life's dangers, toil, snares—the death of a loved one or the certainty of one's own death? I said earlier that at my age I stop asking questions. The truth is that I do not stop, especially when questions of life confront me. Can we calculate God's dealings? Does grace come as a sudden seizure or slowly as a mist or gentle rain? Does preparation cheapen grace by challenging God's inscrutable will? Life does bring answers, sometimes during the most unlikely circumstances. Suddenly, as was the case with both Paul and Pascal, a light singled them out and a voice spoke to them—and, slowly through the years, to a professor grappling with the very ideas he had challenged his students. His years shaped answers much like the stones that rain and wind and sun continue to carve on Utah's rocks and canyons.

Inner landscapes mark who we are and make authoritative what the apostle Peter called "the hidden person of the heart." Questions and answers derived from the heart's exposure are the ones to which religion gives ultimate importance. Grace is free but does not come cheap. At times life darkens and the traveler needs companions like the Psalmist or Bach. Some people deny the journey or reject the helping hand. The opening lines of John Donne's sonnet announce the paradox:

> Batter my heart, three-personed God; for You
> As yet but knock, breathe, shine, and seek to mend;
> That I may rise, and stand, o'erthrow me, and bend
> Your force, to break, blow, burn, and make me new.

Does grace most surely come when storms rage the fiercest? Is this the paradox of grace: that salvation is born only of utter desperation?

Science does little for the soul and technology even less. Neither originates from the heart nor is empowered from culture including its institutions and markets, laws and customs, computers and satellites. Even words and music and dance—human achievements, powerful to be sure—fail to stanch the bleeding heart. Nothing works its miracle like the Spirit—the "unknowing" which cannot be touched, measured, contained. Its power transcends nature and what the human mind creates. Because such mystery compels our adoration, inspires our faith, heals the heart, and brings the peace, we call it "Holy."

When meditating, I confront the religious dimension implicit in Christian orthodoxy: flesh/spirit (Paul); Fall/rebirth (Augustine); free will/divine grace (Calvin); works/faith (Luther); nature/regeneration (Edwards).

Whether we choose to stand on one side or the other, or simultaneously bestride both—or from indifference choose neither—or with twinge of conscience postpone until tomorrow and tomorrow the necessary choice—or conclude that choice itself is moot, being predestined by the Fall or fate or random chance—we are stuck with the paradox.

Ruminations finally bring me back to the door that can be both opened or closed, to the person who enters or exits.

Late on winter afternoons when darkness comes early, I often sat alone in the church sanctuary. The staff had gone home. So very quiet, vacant, the church at dusk became my own inner sanctuary where I might hear some sound, some voice within or beyond the silence. The pews face west. Central on the wall is a grand window, its stained glass replete with golden color if sunset has its way. It's hardly like the reds and blues that blaze in the west window of France's Chartres cathedral. But the one that fronts me in this time-worn place does its own beautiful thing to what's inside me. Here I know peace and know the paradox too: that this light, this grace sent from the outside requires I first come inside to behold it.

Closing

THIS BOOK'S "Opening" recalls the vesper service I once attended in London's Westminster Abbey. My eyes repeatedly focused on the words "Born" and "Died" chiseled into the stone slab beneath my chair, the only words surviving centuries of footsteps. Other words and dates have disappeared into eternal mystery. Ruminations now remind me that my birth originates in mystery and death returns me to it. We return from whence we came.

In "Closing" I think again of John's gospel, the most mystical, the most poetic of the four. His narrative that includes Jesus' birth and death—his birth pre-historical from the world's "beginning" and his death a prelude ("I go to prepare a place")—reaches eerie sublimity. John's first eighteen verses comprise a haunting poem, and throughout the gospel his very words touch ever deeper meanings:

> *temple*: "Destroy this [Jerusalem?] temple and in three days I will raise it up" (2:19).
> *water*: "living water . . . whoever drinks . . . will never thirst" (4:10, 14).
> *bread*: "food which endures to eternal life" (6:22).
> *sleep*: Lazarus "sleeps" (already four days in his tomb); "I go to him out of sleep" (11:11).

John's Jesus strives to identify himself: "I am the good shepherd" (10:14); "I am the resurrection and the life" (11:25); "I am the vine" (15:5). But few if any listeners understand. He explains to the high priest Annas, "I have spoken openly to the world; I have said nothing secretly," (18:20). As his days shorten he promises his disciples that he will stop speaking in metaphors, symbols, parables: "I shall no longer speak to you in figures [of speech] but tell you plainly of the Father" (16:25). However, the more he explains himself, the more mystifying his efforts and the more certain his failure.

The gospel's structure, tone, texture, indeed its mounting drama, compels our attention. So astonishing the miracles and ominous the impending conflict that we suspend our disbelief in order to believe the text. We sense John's inspired power emanating from a transcendental source. His gospel (*god*/good + *spell*/tale) takes us beyond reason and logic, beyond history to the spirit. His words herald the grace-ful gift of love, a reality we see only dimly in this world, know only in part, but someday will behold "face to face" and understand "fully."

Coursing through John's entire narrative is paradox:

tragedy/divine comedy
unbelief/belief
this world/the next
in/out
birth/death
death/birth
enslavement/freedom

Each component has its claim, its legitimate authority, its separate identity held together not in synthesis but ambiguity and paradox. To overlook this feature is to simplify, narrow, even negate the mystery woven throughout the story. For example: When asked by the father to heal his epileptic son "if you can," Jesus, obviously piqued, said, "If you can! [!]." The question should have been "will you" not "can you," the father speaking from faith not doubt. But the good man goes no further than the paradox, "I believe; help my unbelief" (Mark 9:24).

Nowadays, I find most relevant the paradox that balances boundaries, law, and mortality with freedom, the same freedom Jesus announces to his disciples: "The truth shall make you free"

(John 8:31). While shackled, Paul exalts freedom that comes "in the law of the Spirit" (Romans 8:2) by which he means the "law of love," which itself is paradoxical. We hear Martin Luther King's forever-echoing words, "Free at last, free at last. Thank God Almighty, I'm free at last!"—even while he foreknows his death close at hand.

I've lived my life—no need to fuss over vitamins, exercise, or weight, ponder "recent studies" proffered by the *New England Journal of Medicine*, or dose on drugs and faraway travel. I've been blessed by parental love, marriage, and two sons and a daughter. Blessings range beyond number: love, adventure, challenge, sacrifice, heartache, joy. . . . Still more: travel, music, poetry, landscapes of beauty and awe.

"Thank you, God, for life's fullness—for the freedom to be all I have been given and have become, by your grace." Now, like ink on a page too long in sunlight, the loyalty this world demands fades. Flesh holds no dominion, mortality no crown. Scars remain, making clarion the trumpet voice of freedom.

Suddenly, the doctor's phone call confirming *cancer* and forcing *my* slow but necessary acceptance of *my* mortality. The biopsy gave hints of a strange new freedom. Not freedom that annuls the cancer. Earth is still earth; humanity, humanity; death, death—no rainbow without the mist, no joy without the tears, no Benedictus and Pacem without first the Kyrie and Misere. My little universe whispers to me: flesh withers, but the soul wakens to wander, wonder. Horizons dawn luminous as I edge toward death's abyss.

Now, from T. S. Eliot come the words about the crucified "surgeon" beneath whose "bleeding hands we feel / The sharp compassion of the healer's art / Resolving the enigma of the fever chart." From his piercing love come rescue and release. King had seen the Promised Land, so also the disciple Peter who, when beholding it, shouted "with joy unspeakable and full of glory."

We're created for freedom. While earth-bound we strain our bonds. But when the healer breaks the bonds, we soar in Spirit and in Truth to another Kingdom held within God's all-encircling love. The biopsy breaks me free to see, to be, some day to know the glory and the joy.

www.ingramcontent.com/pod-product-compliance
Lightning Source LLC
Chambersburg PA
CBHW070929160426
43193CB00011B/1624